Beginner's Guide to Basketball

Beginner's Guide to Basketball

Kerry Mumford and
Morris A. Wordsworth

PELHAM BOOKS

First published in Great Britain by
PELHAM BOOKS LIMITED
52 Bedford Square
London WC1B 3EF
JULY 1974
SECOND IMPRESSION MARCH 1976

ISBN 0 7207 0740 4

Printed in Great Britain by
Hollen Street Press Ltd at Slough
and bound by James Burn at Esher, Surrey

To Delia

———

To M.M.M.

Contents

List of Illustrations

Acknowledgements

The authors express their grateful thanks to the following for supplying photographs: Dennis Assinder Photographic Studio: 8 and 14; Terry Barnett: 3, 4, 5 and 11; M. D. Griffiths: 9 and 13; (Photographs 1, 2, 6, 7 and 12 were taken by Morris Wordsworth). The authors also extend their thanks to Mrs D. Wordsworth, Doncaster Secretarial Bureau, who typed the manuscript.

Diagrams

Diagrams

Legend for Diagrams

●₄	Attacking player No. 4
■₈	Defending player No. 8
●—→	Movement of player without the ball
●∿∿→	Movement of player dribbling the ball
----→	Movement of ball (pass)
●—(	Attacking player setting a screen
■—┤	Defending player establishing a good defensive position
●•	Position of possible shot by attacking player
●	Numbers attached to passes indicate the sequence of passes

Definition of Terms Used

Pivoting

Rule 7, Article 52 : A pivot takes place when a player who is holding the ball steps once or more than once in any direction with the same foot – the other foot, called the pivot foot, being kept at its point of contact with the floor. (A pivot is used when a player with the ball wishes to change the direction he is facing in order to pass, dribble or to protect the ball from a defender.)

A 'Cut'

A cut is the action of an attacking player who runs quickly towards the basket looking for a pass – usually a return pass.

A 'Fake'

This is a movemet performed by a player with or without the ball, which is meant to deceive an opponent in order to execute a further manoeuvre.

1-on-1

This notation is used to describe the competitive situation of *one attacker* playing against *one defender*. Similarly 2-on-1 would be two attackers against one defender, etc.

Fast Break

A fast break is a team offensive manoeuvre performed immediately after a change of possession in order to advance the ball quickly down court to outnumber the defence within the shooting area.

Attacking Positions
(Diagram 1)

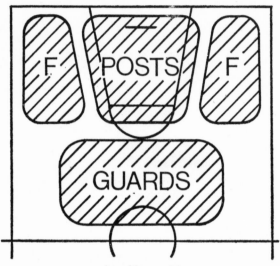

1.   Attacking positions

Guard Position
This is the position in the middle of the court from which an attacking player starts the offensive team manoeuvres. Also known as the rear-court guard area, and at least one player should always be in this area to preserve defensive balance.

Forward Positions
These are the positions in which an attacking player operates on each side of the court between the restricted area and the sideline.

Post Position
This is the position in which an attacking player is in close proximity to the basket (in and around the restricted area).

1. *The Development and Introduction of The Game*

RECENT DEVELOPMENTS IN ENGLISH BASKETBALL

Many words have been written on the history of the game and it is not the intention to write about this again. What is important is that readers should know that basketball is *played* and *watched* by more people throughout the world today than any other game. It is also important to highlight some recent developments in this country to show how the game is growing.

The development of basketball in England was hampered by lack of facilities and equipment, but this barrier has now been removed with the building of sports halls and centres throughout the country by Local Authorities. Now that the game can be played in its proper form, instead of in a 70 x 40 ft. gymnasium, it will develop in spectator appeal, in playing standards, and in the number of participants.

The signs of development in any game are indicated mainly in in the competitive levels and standards of its younger players. In this country the history of the English Schools Basket Ball Association will show what very good progress has been made by these younger players. It was formed in 1957 with eight local Basket Ball Associations. In 1958 the Under 15 National Competition was started. By 1974 the English Schools Basket Ball Association was running ten National Competitions for both boys and girls for the local Basket Ball Associations and individual schools. The National Individual Schools Competition with its complementary Plate Competition had 253 schools taking part, and shows an annual increase of about 25 per cent. Internationally, too, the E.S.B.B.A. runs teams for both boys and girls at Under 18 and Under 16 levels. In addition, the National Individual Schools Champions take part in the Pan European Schools Championships. The hotbeds of school basketball also keep changing, which is a very encouraging sign for it shows that improvement is nationwide and therefore has a beneficial effect on the whole game. In the early stages, players for the International Schools' teams came mainly from London. In recent years the emergence of players from Liverpool, Manchester and more recently Birmingham and Walsall has encouraged other areas. Now the International teams are made up of players from all parts of the country, with individuals from East Kent, Devon and the North-East pushing for International places at Schools' level.

In 1971 The English Mini Basketball Association was formed, and now we have players in the 9 to 13 year age group being introduced into the game.

At adult level, too, there have been major developments to stimulate interest and participation. Our major domestic clubs have stopped being beaten easily in the first round of the European Cup competitions. In recent years both Sutton, Avenue along with Turnford Tigers, the National Women's Champions, have got through their first-round ties commendably. These achievements show that the standard of our top domestic clubs is improving at a relatively quick rate. Other signs internationally have been the performances of the Great Britain team in the Pre-Olympic Tournament in 1972, and more particularly the England team in the European Championships and the British Universities in the World Student Games in Moscow during 1973. As Coach Vic Ambler remarked on his return from these Championships, 'The Europeans now regard us as a middle order team and not a bottom order team'. The National Junior Team has in recent years returned from the Dr Albert Schweitzer International Junior Tournament in Mannheim, Germany, with an ever-increasing number of victories under its belt.

On the domestic scene, there has been the growth of the regional leagues such as the Central League founded in 1969 and more recently the Southern League and Northern League.

With the growth of these leagues it was apparent that a nationwide league was in demand, and in 1972 the National Basketball League was formed by the Amateur Basket Ball Association with the full resources of the administrative offices behind
it.

This gave it the efficiency to ensure the commendable success
that it proved with only six teams taking part to begin with.
Due to this success, the National League has expanded, which
enables young players all over the country to see the top players
in action at the promotions staged in their areas. Details of the
matches in the current season can be obtained from the Amateur
Basket Ball Association's administrative office.

A further important aspect which will aid the development
of playing standards is the setting up of many summer camps
for young players. These camps are run by top coaches and
take place in various parts of the country. The best known one
was run by the Bracknell Sports Centre and others are developing in Essex, Brighton and the North. They give young players
one or two weeks' concentrated playing and coaching, in addition to opportunities for seeing players of International standard
in action and playing with them.

All these instances of development show what a tremendous
effort has been made throughout the country by players, coaches
and administrators in recent years for the good of the game.
Their efforts have been duly rewarded by bringing the game up
to the relatively healthy state that it is in today – a position
which it can build on and expand even more.

INTRODUCING THE GAME

One aspect of basketball which can always be improved is that
concerned with its introduction to beginners and the progressions
and improved technical standards as the players gain in
experience.

The modern game has a tremendous amount to offer, not
only as a major game in its own right, but also as a means of
general games education. In schools and youth establishments it
has this dual-purpose role, for it contains the rudiments in

most forms of all other major winter games such as soccer, rugby, hockey and netball. Since these are outdoor sports and depend upon our undependable weather, basketball should be given considerable space in any planning of indoor winter activities.

Unfortunately, in the past there have not been the indoor facilities to utilise, but as stated previously this excuse has largely disappeared. Also the methods used tended to discourage young players, for they gave the impression that the game was slow and lacking in freedom of individual expression.

Today's game is fast and furious; it demands physical effort to produce the speed at which it should be played and an increasing level of skill to utilise the openings which are made. There is greater reliance on the individual to dribble and score – something else which has been actively discouraged in the past. The 'pride' of individual defensive ability, too, is something which will appeal to those who are anxious to show their physical attributes. As for general games education, there is the opportunity to learn the principles of progressing the ball, and the ways and means of utilising players and spaces to establish principles of penetration without having to contend with the difficult specific actions required to play the other games.

It is therefore relevant at this stage to give some description of the game which will have an effect on the analysis of it when teachers and coaches wish to continue and improve their knowledge.

Basketball is a running game, where a team attempts to get the ball, and more players than their opponents have, at the scoring end, in order to facilitate a score. The individual skills used are dribbling (running with the ball), passing and shooting, generally in that order. The methods used to progress the ball and penetrate are the utilisation of spaces and the utilisation of other players and are called Pre-Tactical Skills. So far we may have been talking about any game, and this is all to the good for it shows that there are common principles. More specific, however, are the team and tactical skills which every game has and which are generally peculiar to that game.

After this brief description the next item is: 'What are the stages of introduction?' Every child has *some* ball-handling skill so the first stage of introduction must always be to let the child play. Later in this chapter two examples will be given of how it is possible to get children playing the game in its basic form within minutes; and this initial play is very important, for it is from it that their future interest in the game will stem. It is also desirable that, in conjunction with this, children should see the game being played at its highest level, and now that the National League is operating this should not prove too difficult. Apart from that there are some very good films and film loops available.

At the point where it is obvious that improved technical ability would increase the enjoyment of the participants, that is the time when teaching and coaching should begin. There are many aspects of technical ability, and the teacher will find that abilities of 'how' and 'when', together with establishment of principles of progression and penetration, all develop in accord with each other. Suggestions of order of importance can be made, but these will not satisfy everyone. However, from the text it will be obvious what the authors have found to be successful.

When introducing the game for the first time the players must know what the game is about and what the rules are. On the question of rules, however many the rule book says there are three basic rules to play to. Some are rules to equate the offence and defence in such things as physical stature and equality of opportunity. The rest are to tidy up the administration of the game.

Therefore an introduction could be :

1. Objective To shoot the ball down through the opponents' basket.

2. Method To pass or dribble the ball to a position where the Objective can be easily achieved.

3. Rules (a) There will be no contact between opponents.
(b) When receiving the ball a player is

allowed ONE pace to steady himself or to turn in another direction.

(c) A player cannot run with the ball unless it is bounced. Having finished bouncing it, a player may not start off again.

ADMINISTRATIVE NOTES

When a score is made the defending team throws the ball in from the end line. The game is continuous. When rules are broken or the ball goes out, the non-responsible team throws it in from the nearest point at the side.

Two useful and proven ways of introduction, after explanation of the rules, are as follows :

METHOD 1

ORGANISATION

Teams of 2, each team in a distinctive coloured bib, viz. 2 Reds, 2 Greens, 2 Blues, 2 Whites, 2 Yellows, 2 Blanks.

Having explained the rules, Reds play Greens, Blues play Whites, Yellows play Blanks, *all at the same time,* utilising the whole court and each game starting at one of the circle spots with the ball being thrown up by one of the players. After a score, the game continues with the non-scoring team throwing the ball in from the scoring end.

ADMINISTRATIVE NOTES

This form of game with two per team is most suitable for absolute beginners.

Constant reminder of the rules is required.

It has been found that bibs are better than coloured bands, as the colour mass is more easily recognisable.

The games can take place quite easily within a 20 metre length floor, and if a sports hall is available then three sets of games are easily fitted in across the width of a hall.

If only one court is available, then the number of persons per colour is doubled and 2 Reds play against 2 Reds. A player with the ball then only has to recognise his team-mate's face out of the other three of the same colour. On a 60 x 40 ft. court this method has been used satisfactorily for up to six games at once (24 players) with constant reminders on the 'no contact rule' and 'look where you are going'. It has also been used in conjunction with method 2.

Method 2

ORGANISATION

Teams of 3 or 4, dependent upon class numbers and size of court(s) available, each team being in distinctly coloured shirts or bibs. Having explained the rules, the game between two teams is started from the centre circle. Whoever scores first stays on the court and immediately plays away from the scoring end.

The losers go off behind the queue, which is formed by the other teams at the side of the court.

The losers are replaced by the team at the head of the queue, who go on to defend. Another game is then in progress immediately. The process is repeated every time there is a score.

ADMINISTRATIVE NOTES

If there is no score after one minute of play, both teams retire behind the queue and a new game is started at the centre circle between the first two teams in the queue.

The head of the queue is always at the mid point of the sideline.

If a team wins three consecutive games then that team comes off court and the losers stay on, thus preventing a monopoly.

Once the organisation is established in the players minds, the coach may find it useful to let the team coming on throw the ball in after a score, but care should be taken that only 5 seconds elapse between a basket scored and the ball thrown in again from the scoring end.

Certain other rules can be introduced by the coach to bring the method into line with the game proper and also to give better organisation.

The advantages of this method are :

1. Using the three courts across a sports hall or large gym, the number of players per team and number of teams can be adjusted to cater for up to 48 players quite easily.

2. The last team in the queue can be responsible for refereeing and timing, leaving the teacher to coach.

3. The immediate turn-round after scoring injects a sense of speed into the game.

4. It gives the 3-on-3 situation, which is beneficial for all levels of play.

5. As each team comes off, it registers the number of games won on a scoreboard. Winning three in a row scores a bonus.

These two methods are only suggested as guide lines, and teachers should change and adopt them according to their own facilities and equipment.

Both methods will provide easy opportunities for playing the game in its basic form; but although younger players may experience some initial difficulties in understanding the organisation, once this has been established the methods can be used for evermore where numbers are a problem, no matter what level of ability one is dealing with. Method 2 has been particularly useful in teaching the Fast Break and also the very first stages of a Pressing Defence after a score.

With the game introduced and the players learning its basic principles, this is the point where teaching really begins : in subsequent chapters those technical aspects which add to the enjoyment and success of the participants are dealt with in an order which can be used as a guide. Practices are generally listed in a progressive order.

2. *Individual Offensive Skills*

TEACHING CONSIDERATIONS

This book will not contain everything there is to know about basketball; it is necessary, therefore, that some information be given about the teaching of skills so that the reader may be more familiar with the approach and methods used. He will, from this information, be able to understand more fully the progressions used to adopt a consistent form for teaching aspects which arise which have not been covered.

A skill contains three inter-related facets. These facets are Technique, Timing and Situation. A skilful player knows *which* skill to perform (Situation), how to perform it (Technique), and when to do it (Timing). These facets must be developed in accord with each other. At the same time, however, it must be remembered that one should ONLY *teach one thing at a time.* Very often practices can be multi-purpose, in which case the teacher or coach should be careful to concentrate on only the one aspect which he is trying to develop in the players at that time. This does not mean that major fundamental errors should not be corrected when they arise.

Due to the inter-relationship of all three facets, game skills are taught in small 'game situation' activities. This term can be grossly misused and often teachers do not understand its function. A 'game situation' should be an activity which contains all three facets mentioned above, but two of the facets are controlled whilst the other one is developed. In other words, teaching still takes place and learning is not purely incidental. A good 'game situation' will be adjustable to allow for the execution of a performance whatever the standard of the performer. The adjustment is on the amount of defensive pressure which is applied and/or the amount of space available to the performer. This has particular relevance when one considers that players learn by *trial* and *success* and not by trial and error, as is so often quoted. Again, in the 'game situation' the amount of activity a learner is expected to undertake and the amount of pressure applied upon him, will be regulated in order to provide that success. As the performance improves so will the pressure be increased, but never so much as to impede the 60 to 70 per cent success rate. If the rate is below this level, then the pressure of time and/or space is too high; and conversely if it is above this level, the pressure is not high enough.

When designing practices for the teaching of skills, care should be taken that the actual performance bears relation to the way those skills are performed in the game; for it is no use practising one way and playing another. Practices also have to make maximum use of the facilities and equipment available, and be progressive and rotational in order to allow for maximum participation.

Having said these things about the teaching of skills, every effort should be made to allow the performer to play the game proper, for this is the only way that 'real' success can be measured.

GETTING FREE TO RECEIVE

In the modern game, where defence is played all over the court, getting free is the first thing a player has to learn. Whilst all skills are important, this particular skill is perhaps the one which enables the player to take a more prominent role in the game. It enables him always to be a threat. It is not enough to be able to catch the ball. A player must be able to catch it *and* be in a position to do something positive and constructive with it. He should have space and time to turn and face the basket in order to shoot, or to drive, or to pass to someone else who is in a better position to shoot or to drive.

Getting free requires the attacking player to out-manoeuvre his opponent in order to create space, and therefore time. He will usually receive the ball on the side away from the defender. To out-manoeuvre another player requires a change of direction and a change of pace. This can be interpreted as doing the opposite to the opponent – if the opponent stands still the attacker moves, if the opponent moves to follow, the attacker goes back the other way, or checks his movement, and accelerates the same way. To do this effectively the learner should watch the defender (opponent) and not watch the ball, until such progress has been made that watching both is possible. This can be accomplished by not having the ball passed between players until the out-manoeuvring is complete and the receiver signals that he is free to receive the ball. By showing the hand, it not only acts as a signal of freedom, but also indicates a target to the passer. In order to make the 'getting free' more pronounced, the pass used in this operation should be from the chest area in front of the body. Overhead and bounce passes should be forbidden at this stage.

PRACTICES FOR GETTING FREE TO RECEIVE

1. PIG IN THE MIDDLE – all over the court.
Check points
* Watch the defender (opponent).
* Signal when free.
* Pass and move.
* Pass only when you see the signal.

2. The same 'PIG IN THE MIDDLE' activity with a time limit before the ball can be passed. A count of 3 seconds will give the 'pig' more time to get to the free player, and also make the free player work harder. The 'pig' should be encouraged to defend the receiver. The same check points apply.

3. The 'PIG IN THE MIDDLE' activity is slightly modified by transferring it to the basket area and by having predetermined starting positions (see Diagram 2). This is an exercise in passing between GUARD and FORWARD positions. The pass from the GUARD starts the process. The GUARD must stay where he is.

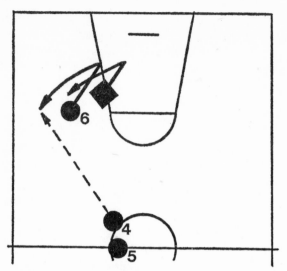

2. 'Pig in the middle' with predetermined starting positions

The receiver makes a shot when he gets the ball. If he is unable to make a shot, then he can return the ball, and continue to get free and receive until such time as he is able to make a shot.

Check points

* After receiving the ball sideways, *pivot* to get feet parallel.

(a) on front foot if you have space.

(b) on back foot if you do not have enough space.

The practice is made rotational *after a shot* by the following changes. The GUARD moves to the FORWARD position, the FORWARD becomes the DEFENDER, and the DEFENDER, who should get the rebound, passes the ball to the front man in the QUEUE and then joins the queue. The process starts again.

Transfering this practice to the basket area adds the additional dimension of 'direction'; for it will determine more effectively the side on which it will be received, and also indicate that the receiver has to turn to the basket in order to make the shot. With not very able performers, the distance between the starting positions of the FORWARD and DEFENDER can be increased thus making it easier to achieve success. Teachers can vary this distance according to abilities up to the point where, with proficient players, only the Guards position is predetermined.

CATCHING

Because the game is played at speed, the ball will be caught on the move more often than it is caught standing still. It is very rare that the ball will come straight to the person receiving it in front of the chest. A detailed look at playing situations in the game shows that it is either caught at the side or over the head. The catching techniques then are not to reach for the ball with two hands, but to place the hand on the receiving side in a position to stop the ball's forward motion, and use the other hand to give a vice-like grip. Both hands are then used to bring the ball to a position for the next movement. For catching, the coaching is done in conjunction with 'Getting Free to Receive'.

Check points
* Reach with the hand.
* Spread the hand and make it the same shape as the ball.
* Use both hands to hold the ball and bring it under control.

PASSING

The pass involves two people and therefore communication, as mentioned in the section on receiving the ball. It is just as important when projecting the ball in order to make sure the ball reaches its desired target. Passing techniques are designed to give an efficient projection and to uphold certain principles in order to produce a successful result. When the receiver is free to receive the ball, the passer still has to get the ball past his own defender. He will select one of the openings which are available to him, but at the same time be appreciative of the situation around the receiver.

Having selected which pass to make, the technique should allow the pass to get past the defender before he has time to react and close the opening, and also get the ball to the receiver as quickly as possible in order to give him the advantages of time and space. Movement of the ball should be instantaneous in the direction in which it is to go and should be with force. Short- and medium-range passes should be with two hands. There should be no flexion of the elbows when the pass is made, only a forceful extension. Passes to the side of a defender are made from in front of the body, and passes over the defender are made from a position above the head.

The longer passes are generally made with one hand and the technique for this is similar to throwing any implement, except that the hand is stretched out behind the ball.

Technique is geared to producing a quick straight ball to up-hold the principle of shortest distance, fastest time.

The Bounce Pass is used by the passer who is on the move and it is adopted for a number of reasons : firstly, because the passer has not enough time to lift the ball up to a two-handed overhead position before the chance of a pass is lost (e.g. Guard to Post or Forward to Post), and secondly, because the receiver's defender is in the way of a front pass. In the case of the Guard or Forward to Post it is a legitimate excuse, but in the latter case it is not. It means that the receiver has not got free enough, and when he receives the ball he is under too much pressure anyway. Bounce passing should be discouraged rather than encouraged with beginners.

PRACTICES FOR FRONT PASS
1. 'Pig in the middle' all over the court.
Check points
* Force the ball away.
* Step towards the receiver with the non-pivot foot.
2. 3-on-2 all over the court.
3. See progression (3) on page 25 of 'Getting Free to Receive'.

PRACTICES FOR OVERHEAD PASS
1. 'Pig in the middle' with a time count of 3 seconds before the ball is passed. The opponent should defend only the player with the ball. The time count would allow for time to do this.

Check points

* Hold the ball up as soon as it is received.

* No backward motion of the ball before projection.

* If the defender overcrowds, keep one foot still and turn away bringing the ball down. Wait for the receiver to find a new position.

NOTE. It is at this point that pivoting comes into its own.

2. 3-on-2 all over the court.

PRACTICES FOR BOTH TYPES OF PASSES

1. Starting positions as for practice (3) (page 25) of 'Getting Free to Receive'.

The activity is started by a front pass from the Guard to the Forward. The Forward can now shoot or use an overhead pass to the Guard who has cut towards the basket.

The choice will depend upon the position of the defender. If the defender is close, the overhead pass to the Guard is made and the Guard takes a lay-up shot. If the defender sags back to prevent the return pass being made to the Guard, an outside shot is taken. The rotation of players is exactly as before: Guard to Forward, Forward to Defender, Defender passes the ball to front of queue and goes behind it.

2. A game of 3-on-3, starting from the half-way line and finishing with a shot. If there are a number of groups, then the following organisation at one end of the court can be used: Group A to attack, Group B to defend, Group C and D, etc. to wait at the mid point of the sideline. After a score or loss of possession, Group A become defenders, Group C attack and Group B join the queue at the half-way line.

SHOOTING

It is impossible to win the game without good percentage shooting. Good percentage shooting relies on technique, positioning and confidence which is built upon success. It is most important, therefore, in the teaching of shooting that a high success rate is allowed for in the practices used.

THE JUMP SHOT

The main shot of the game is the Jump Shot and this shot should be taught first. The execution of the Jump Shot needs a well-balanced body position, although when the shot is perfected body control is the major factor. Many top shooters today do not shoot from a well-balanced position, but they do have an exceptional degree of body control which stems from such a position.

In teaching the beginner, care must be taken to establish a *close* position to the basket with a ball which is not too heavy. As the technique is learned, the distance and the weight of the ball can be increased accordingly. It should be remembered that a mini basketball with its relevant weight is recommended for children from 9–13 years old.

The technique requires the ball to be taken from the holding position in front of the body to a position where it is held on one hand above the head. The other hand is held at the side of the ball to steady it. The shooting action is then to extend the elbows and wrist and push the ball in an arc towards the basket.

PRACTICES TO ESTABLISH THE INITIAL TECHNIQUE OF THE JUMP SHOT

1. Each payer with a ball standing in a semi-circle approx $1\frac{1}{2}$ metres from the basket. Each player should be facing the basket in a well-balanced position. Those players who do not have a ball stand inside the semi-circle to retrieve for those that do.

Players with a ball shoot in their own time, shooting directly into the basket.

Check points
* Feet slightly apart pointing towards the basket.
* Take the ball to a position above the head so that the shooting arm has :
  (a) the elbow pointing to the basket,
  (b) fingers spread, pointing backwards,
  (c) the ball resting on the whole of the hand and fingers,
  (d) wrist cocked.
* Shoulders square to the basket.
* Use the other hand to steady the ball on the side.

* Push the ball toward the basket.
* Knees straight to prevent forward motion.
* Signal to the retrievers for the ball.

NOTE : NO JUMPING AT THIS STAGE.

2. The same activity but players work in two's. The retriever in this instance stands approximately 30 cm. in front of the shooter with his arms together and *vertical* in line with the ball and basket. When the shooter shoots he does *not* attempt to block the shot. With his arms raised he assists the shooter considerably to establish a suitable trajectory for the ball.

Without this help the shooter would shoot far too flat. The 'defender' retrieves the ball immediately the shot is taken, passes it to the shooter and establishes position again. The shooter takes at least six shots before the pairs change over. The check points are as for the previous activity but shooters should be encouraged not to move their initial position.

3. The same activity, but the shooter's position is about a metre farther from the basket (2½ metres) and is made a little competitive. The retriever should pass the ball from under the basket area and then approach the shooter to block the shot. As soon as the shot is taken he must retrieve the ball again. At least six attempts are taken.

Check points

* Technique.
* Use the legs to give added power.

4. The same practice as for 3 with the shooter a little farther away from the basket. In addition, the shooter is instructed to shoot using a little jump. As the players get more proficient, so the height of their jump will increase. Progression can be fairly quick, but standards should not be sacrificed.

Check points

* Shoot high for the ball to drop into the basket.
* Jump straight up – don't jump forward.

THE LAY-UP SHOT

The other main shot in the game is the 'lay-up' shot. Arguments have raged over a long period of time as to whether this shot should be taught first or not. Analysis of schools basketball shows that there are many more opportunities for the jump shot than the lay-up shot and this would tend to indicate priorities. In addition, there is easier transference from the jump shot to the lay-up shot than vice versa. The way to teach the lay-up shot is to demonstrate it and then let the beginner try it. If a good demonstration is given, then most beginners will be able to copy it. If they are not getting the success that is expected, then reference should be made to the *check* points following.

PRACTICES FOR THE LAY-UP SHOT

1. A queue of an odd number of players on the right-hand side of the court together with odd numbers in possession of a ball. Using a half-court only, the player dribbles, shoots, leaves the ball and joins the end of the queue. The player behind him follows, secures the ball after the shot and dribbles to the back of the queue. He now has a ball and the player behind him does not have one. The process is repeated and is continuous. Players must stay in their original order. The activity can be started on the left-hand side of the court later, to develop ambidexterity. The same practice can be conducted around each basket.

2. *An alternative method:* Two queues of odd numbers of players, one each side of the court, facing in opposite directions. The odd numbered players in each queue should have a ball. The first player in each queue dribbles to the basket and shoots, leaves the ball and joins the end of the queue on the opposite side of the court. The player behind him follows, secures the ball after the shot, and joins the other queue, now having a ball in his possession. The others follow on accordingly. The circularisation can be reversed to develop ambidexterity.

NOTE : For this practice an even number of players in the class is required. The teacher can join in the activity to make the even number.

Check points
* Jump high from near to the basket.
* Hand behind the ball.

* Put the ball on the backboard on the small vertical line at the side of the basket.

If the teacher finds that some pupils still have difficulty, then it is suggested that Method 1 be used, but the dribble is left out in one group until the other points have been mastered.

3. The 'lay-up' drill which is commonly used with slight variations is recommended as the next step. It involves a pass to the corner and a return pass to the shooter (see Diagram 3, top half).

4. This progression involves catching the ball coming from behind and then continuing with a dribble and shot whilst being chased (see Diagram 3, bottom half).

FREE-THROW SHOOTING

Shooting Free-Throws is a ritual. It is purely a technique which the player has to perform whilst withstanding psychological pressure. Everything in the performance should be controlled in a methodical way so that it can be repeated ad infinitum, whatever the time span between the sets of shots. The technique used is that used for the jump shot without the jump. Complete concentration is required on the job in hand. A suggested ritual is:

(1) Receive the ball from the referee.
(2) Check the feet positioning.
(3) Adjust the hand grip.
(4) Go to the shooting position with ball above the head.
(5) Shoot.

PRACTICE FOR FREE-THROW SHOOTING

Free-shooting competitions between players where shots are taken in pairs – usually after vigorous activity.

Check points
* As for the technique of shooting.
* Think of the ritual.

DRIBBLING

The dribble is used as an alternative means of progressing the ball towards the basket. There are clearly defined rules about

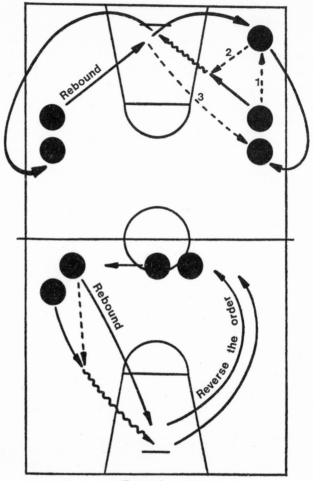

3.   'Lay-up' practices

dribbling and these should be introduced and complied with during teaching sessions, though during games, particularly for the not so able participant, excessive halting of the game is detrimental. That is not to say that gross abuse of the rules should be allowed.

The rules which are to be complied with are :

(1) The ball must be going downwards before the pivot foot leaves the floor.

(2) When the dribbler stops he must not take more than one pace with the ball at rest in his hands.

(3) Whilst dribbling, the ball must not be projected horizontally.

(4) After the dribble comes to an end, that is to say the ball comes to rest in *one or two* hands, the player may not dribble again without first regaining possession.

Dribbling is the only ball-handling skill where possession is retained and therefore provides an activity which beginners find more motivating. It is important that during teaching periods in the early stages, viz. during the games indicated in Chapter 1, the teacher does NOT dispense with the dribble, but has other ways of controlling its excessive use. A suggested method of control is to allow the dribble in a direct straight line only towards the basket. Any deviation from this straight line should be considered a transgression of the 'Teachers' Rule'. It means that right from the start players are using the dribble for its intended purpose, but the moment there is someone in the way, the dribbler has to stop, hold the ball up and shoot or, more likely, pass.

The technique of dribbling requires as much of the hand to be placed on the ball as possible. The hand should be spread and an attempt made to shape it to the circumference of the ball. The bouncing of the ball is achieved by movement of the elbow, wrist and fingers. After projecting the ball downwards, the hand is then in a position to receive it back again, taking the pace off the ball and starting a further bounce. In order to change the pace and direction of the ball quickly, the time between bounces should be short and players must therefore stoop to get the hand lower. Care must be taken, however, to ensure that players continue to look forward whilst dribbling and not at the ball. By looking forward they will not miss the opportunity of passing forward to a team-mate who is in a position to score.

PRACTICES FOR DRIBBLING

1. A game called 'robbers'. Two-thirds of the class with a *ball each* begin dribbling within specified areas, usually the basket-

ball court. The other third then have to 'steal' a ball from the dribblers without touching anybody. If the ball goes outside the court or the dribbler stops dribbling, it must be given to the nearest player without a ball.

Check points
* Spread the hand to the shape of the ball.
* Keep the bounces short.
* 'Look up to see where the robbers are.'
* Dribble away quickly.

2. The same activity, but more aggression induced by having a forfeit for those players who do not have a ball after a time lapse (usually 10 second intervals).

Check points
* Use the body to protect the ball.
* Change hands when the robber comes round the side.
* Change hands when reversing direction.

3. Practice 3 for 'lay-up' shooting.

DRIVING

Driving is the term used when a dribbler attempts to go straight to the basket either unhindered or by dribbling past an opponent.

DRIVING MANOEUVRES

When driving around opposition there are certain additional skills which will help the driver. Firstly there is the 'change of direction'. In this the offensive player attempts to dribble to the side of the opponent. When the opponent moves across to block the space, the dribbler quickly switches the ball in front of himself to the other hand and drives down the other side.

Secondly there is the 'offensive roll'. In this the attacker again attempts to dribble past the defensive player, but as the defensive player moves to close the gap the attacker places his body in between ball and opponent, changes his dribbling hand and reverses direction, continuing to dribble down the other side of the opponent.

The difference in use of the two methods is that the 'change of direction' is used when the defender reacts early, and the 'offensive roll' is used when the defender reacts late. In both cases, if the defender only moves slightly the driving player will accelerate on the intended original path.

PRACTICES FOR CHANGE OF DIRECTION
1. The players line up as in Diagram 4. O5 has the ball and dribbles two-thirds of the way across the court, stops and passes to O6 and stays there. O6 dribbles with his right hand towards

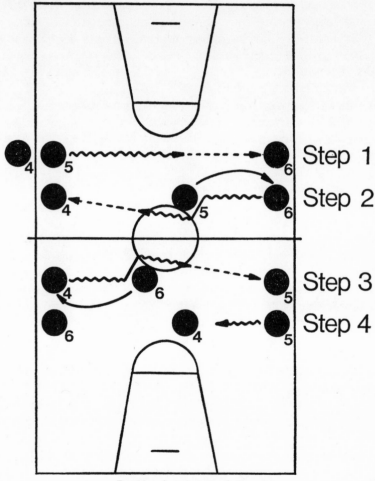

4. Practice for change of direction

O5 on the right-hand side and close. As he approaches O5 he changes hand and direction, and dribbles down the left-hand side with left hand stopping at two-thirds distance.

Immediately O6 gets past O5, O5 takes O6's spot on the side.

The process is then repeated continuously.

Check points

*   Approach cautiously, switch hands, accelerate.

*   Look forward all the time.

2. Same activity, but start with opposite hand to go down left-hand side.

3. Same activity, but have the centre man step to the ball with furthest foot – i.e. step to left with right foot or vice versa as the driver is approaching. This is the signal for the driver to change hands and direction.

4. Allow the driver to approach with either hand.

5. Allow centre man to decide whether to step or not. This gives the choice to the driver of changing when the centre man steps, or of accelerating down the same side if he does not.

PRACTICES FOR OFFENSIVE ROLL

1. The players line up again as in diagram 4 with O5 having the ball.

O5 dribbles two-thirds of the way across the court and stops, passes the ball to O6 and stays there. O6 dribbles with the right hand to the right-hand side of O5 until almost level with him. He reverses his direction and hand, and dribbles down the left-hand side of O5 stopping at two-thirds distance.

Immediately O6 has passed O5, O5 takes O6's place on the side and the process is repeated continuously.

Check points

*   Approach cautiously and accelerate out.

*   Look up all the time.

NOTE : When the dribbling hand is changed, care has to be taken that the dribbling rules are not contravened, particularly those concerned with holding the ball in two hands and holding it underneath – at rest – with one hand. The ball should be in permanent motion. Practices 2, 3 and 4 are similar to those for 'change of direction' in that they use the opposite starting hand.

When the centre man is asked to step across, he should do it with the NEAREST FOOT.

PRACTICES FOR BOTH ACTIVITIES

1. 1-on-1 half court, finishing with a shot. Two sets at a time.
2. 1-on-1 full court, finishing with a shot. Two sets at a time.
3. 1-on-1 full court continuously (i.e. one-man team games) all sets at the same time.

OFFENCE WITHOUT THE BALL

Offence without the ball is something which does not receive attention at all in many coaching sessions and yet it occupies four-fifths of the offensive players' time. Coaching in this aspect, when done, is usually after the event and for a specific instance. Coaches would be better instilling certain ideas into players, particularly during the coaching of the ball-handling skills and during game situation practices where it becomes a relevant exercise.

The items to coach in 'offence without the ball' are numerous. The offensive player can get free to receive, as the defenders usually play 'basket side'; then, being free, he will either be nearer to the basket or farther away from it than the defender. Being farther away but within shooting distance has certain advantages. It keeps the middle free for driving players and also gives more room for players to cut and receive return passes. Also, anyone who does get the ball in the middle will have more room in which to work. A golden rule for all non-Post players should be : keep out of the middle unless you have the ball and can drive, or you are seeking a return pass.

Rebounding in offence is an item which all offensive players should be aware of. Positioning and team tactics determine which players do actually rebound. The technique requires that the offensive player gets past the defender. This is done by faking a movement one way, and then moving hard towards the desired position.

The rebound can be secured with good timing of the jump and determination to hold the ball with two hands if it is contested. The timing is very important so that the ball can be taken at the maximum jumping height. If the ball is very near to the basket, then instead of securing it the player can 'tip' it into the basket using the fingers. If the ball is not near to the basket, players should be encouraged to secure the ball firmly and go straight back up for a shot.

There are no specific practices for developing offence without the ball, and as already stated the principles should be developed at the same time as other offensive skills. Rebounding is usually dealt with when practising defensive rebounding.

PROGRESSION OF THE BALL – PENETRATION

This is again a section of basketball which young players receive little or no coaching in, and yet they must be able to apply the skills correctly in order to give a greater purpose to what they have already learned. The younger players must be directed, whilst care is taken not to reduce their initiative.

The major objective in offensive play is to score as quickly and as often as possible. Here again the straight line principle of shortest distance, fastest time is applicable. In adopting this principle to utilise their skills most effectively, the players should conform to certain 'Teachers' Rules'. These rules are simple, few in number, and have *no* exceptions to create confusions.

The rules that can be used by the ball-handler in any situation to produce penetration are given below. Teachers when applying the rules over a period of time should not expect to get the full implications of the rules understood immediately; they have to be introduced stage by stage. The implications are important in producing a 'frame of mind' in young players to produce greater effectiveness when they have the ball. Each player, every time he receives the ball, should ask himself the following questions in the order given.

RULE I *Can I shoot and score?*
If the answer is YES, *then do so.*
Considerations for the player are:
(a) Distance from the basket.
(b) Position of the defender.

If the answer is NO, then . . .

RULE 2 *Can I get closer to shoot and score?*

If the anser is YES, *then do so.*

Considerations for the player are :

(a) Is the path to the basket clear?

(b) Is it easy to fake and drive past the opponent?

If the answer is NO, then . . .

RULE 3 *Can I pass to someone else who can shoot and score?*

The implications of the rules are :

RULE 1 The player should always turn to face the basket, so if he answers *yes* the shot can be immediate. If the player is in no position to turn and face the basket because of intensive defensive action, then obviously the answer to the question is *no*. Turning to face the basket should be done *anywhere* on the court. The implication of this is beneficial for all situations.

RULE 2 This question is answered quite easily, for if the player is too far from the basket he will be unable to score.

Because he turns to face the basket as in Rule 1, he will easily be able to see if there is a space in front of him to dribble towards the basket. However small the space is, the dribble forward should be attempted, for this commits an opponent to the player with the ball (see Diagram 5).

The player who does not dribble sees four team-mates and five opponents, a situation in which the opponents have the advantage.

The player who dribbles straight and commits an opponent now sees four team-mates, four opponents, plus creating more space in the middle. When someone comes to challenge him, the dribbler should stop and go to Rule 3 or beat the man on the dribble if it is easy to do so within narrow limits.

RULE 3 As a result of turning to face the basket as in Rule 1, the attacker is more likely to make a pass to someone who is in a good shooting or driving position, if and when the attacker arrives at Rule 3, than the attacker would have been if he had not faced the basket. It will be noted that the Rules imply that players should *shoot, drive straight,* and *pass,* in that order. When these habits have been instilled, the one additional instruction to complement them can then be introduced. This

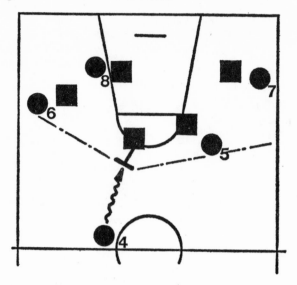

5. Penetration towards the basket

instruction is: *If there is anybody in front of you free – give them the ball.* The reason for doing these things in this order is that if a player is asked to look for passes first, he usually misses easy shooting opportunities and also stands looking for the pass forward, thus wasting a valuable penetration opportunity through not dribbling straight.

When the three rules and the additional instruction are combined, time, distance and valuable scoring opportunities are not wasted and the player develops instincts which help to make an effective team fast break which is highlighted in Chapter 6.

PRACTICES

The teaching of 'progression of the ball' is done entirely in the game and is more effectively done using teams of three. The games played in Method 2 of 'introducing the game' (see page 21) would make it an ideal organisation to use. There are enough players to make it work and enough space on the court for the players themselves to see its effectiveness.

THE I-ON-O SITUATION

The adoption of the three rules makes the beginner able to exploit the 1-on-o situation most effectively without further instruction.

THE I-ON-I SITUATION

This is the basic competitive situation in the game which means that it will be the final progression in the game situations for learning and practising the application of all the individual skills put together. The practice of it is also a form of pressure training for the beginner for shooting and driving. It is so important that this situation be mastered because success at it creates pressure on the team defence, thus making the individual more effective for his team. The ways in which an attacker will succeed at it will depend upon his strengths in the constituent skills and the relative strengths and reactions of the defender.

There are certain additional functions, which are usually performed when playing the 1-on-1 situation, which help the attacking player to be more effective. These are the use of fakes before attempting to shoot, drive or pass, and the use of the dribbling manoeuvres consisting of a change of direction and pace once the dribble has started and becomes a drive.

FAKES

The fake is not an artificial movement, but a movement which is real. If the defensive reaction is quick and effective, the attacker is then able to change his mind and do something else. The original action is then a fake action. If, however, the defensive action is not quick and effective, then the original action should be continued.

The actions available to the attacking player with the ball are :

SHOT

Fake Shot and Shot
Fake Shot and Drive
Fake Shot and Pass

DRIVE

Fake Drive and Shot

Fake Drive and Drive on other side
Fake Drive and Pass

PASS
Fake Pass and Shot
The Fake Shot and Drive is obviously more effective near to the basket since the initial action of the shot does not become a fake if the attacker is out of shooting range. The Fake Drive when the attacker is out of shooting range is more effective than when it is closer to the basket, since the drive to the basket is the most dangerous action outside the 4 metre range. The most common actions are the Shot, Fake Shot and Drive, and Fake Drive to one side and Drive, and Fake Drive to one side and Drive to the other. The action of the Shot has already been described, but the other two need further explanation.

THE FAKE SHOT AND DRIVE
The initial action is as for the shot, viz., receive the ball, pivot to turn and face the basket and attempt the shot. As the ball is being taken up to the shooting position the defender will usually react to stop the shot. It is at this point that the ball is brought back down and the drive started by keeping the pivot foot still and stepping forward with the non-pivot foot, so that on this first stride the non-pivot foot is nearest to the opponent and the dribble will be with the outside hand using the body to protect the ball (see Diagram 6). Correct positioning of the feet all the way through the action will greatly increase the effectiveness.

A good activity for practising the fake shot and drive is practice 3 of 'Getting Free to Receive', with no limitations on the defender. If, of course, the defender does not respond to block the shot, then it is taken. Practice 3 of the 'Jump Shot' is also a useful practice when modified to allow the shooter to jump shoot or lay-up shoot, according to the defender's response to the initial shooting movement.

THE FAKE AND DRIVE
An attempt to drive, from a standing position, is made after the

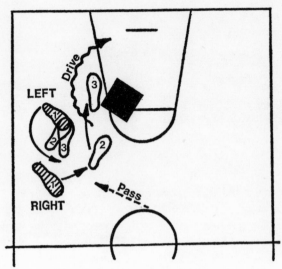

6. The fake shot and drive

ball has been received and the pivot to face the basket has been made. The drive is started by stepping to the left with the left foot, if the left foot is the non-pivot foot, or to the right with the right foot. Half a step is all that is required. The non-pivot foot is then withdrawn and in the same motion placed on the opposite side with the drive commencing immediately, using the outside dribbling hand. Similarly, good footwork in the execution of these movements will increase effectiveness.

Good practices for this particular part have to be controlled carefully. The subject is best dealt with in conjunction with 'defence on the man with the ball' who is outside shooting range. (See the chapter on Defence.)

3. *Individual Defensive Skills*

Before team defence of any kind can be considered, players must be taught individual defence. Too often defence is neglected by teachers and coaches, who tend to spend their entire time working on offence. Half the game is spent on defence, therefore a great deal of time should be devoted to practising defence both individually and collectively. How often have you seen a finely executed offensive manoeuvre resulting in a basket scored, only to see the same player, owing to his poor defensive play, allowing his opposite number to score and even the odds? Players are applauded for their success in offence, and the same recognition should be given to players for their individual defensive skill. The importance of defence should be understood by each individual, who should be taught sound basic movements and be willing to work hard to improve. Players should take pride in their individual defence and feel that this phase of the game is just as much of a challenge as offensive play.

Individual defence is based on the 1-on-1 situation and is designed to discourage or prevent those options available to the offensive player as detailed in Chapter 2. Players should maintain complete body balance, have good footwork to maintain position and make use of their hands and arms to deny or hinder the pass or shot.

DEFENSIVE POSITION

Basic positional play is most important in good defence. To be effective, the player must be in full control of his body at all times and be able to move quickly in any direction – backwards, forwards, laterally and upwards. A good defensive position will vary to meet differing situations. What is termed good for defending a small Guard would not necessarily suffice when defending a tall Post player. Position of the ball will also play an important role in deciding what is the best defensive position to adopt. Is the player being defended in possession of the ball or not? Is he away from the basket or close to the basket? All these factors have to be considered when seeking to apply the correct defence.

Generally speaking, the following factors are needed for good defence:

1. The feet should be comfortably spread in a parallel position, or one foot forward, to give a broad base for good balance.

2. The knees should be bent to keep the body centre of gravity low for mobility and the hips flexed to allow for body movement.

3. The player's head is kept erect, and if he is defending a man without the ball, he should be positioned so as to see both his *man and the ball,* by making use of his peripheral vision. When this is not possible, he should watch the man and not the ball.

4. The arms need to be flexed at the elbows, and when defending a player with the ball his hands should follow the movement of the ball to discourage or prevent the pass or shot.

When playing individual defence, the following situations need to be considered:

(a) Defending a player *with* the ball *away* from the basket.

(b) Defending a player *without* the ball *away* from the basket.

(c) Defending a player *with* the ball *close* to the basket.

(d) Defending a player *without* the ball *close* to the basket.

(e) Blocking out and rebounding when the shot is taken.

Defence Away From the Basket

An attacking player in possession of the ball can shoot, drive or pass, and the objective of the defence is to defend against these in that order of priority. The defender should first take into consideration the attacker's distance from the basket, and if it is seen that he is outside his normal shooting range the defensive requirements are immediately reduced by one-third. This may be even further reduced if the attacker has just completed a dribble and is still outside his shooting range. In this situation the defender should play up close to the attacker (without contact) and harass him into turning his back on the defence in an attempt to protect the ball and/or make him throw a bad pass.

If the attacker has the ball and is within shooting distance, the defender should take up a position to discourage or, better still, deny the shot or drive and force the attacker into passing the ball, but away from the under-basket high-percentage shooting area. This is achieved by adopting the correct defensive position, close enough to pressure the would-be shot, but not so near as to be unable to adjust position if the drive is attempted – usually about 1–1½ metres' distance is sufficient (within touching distance) and the shot is discouraged by use of the hands in the high position. Care must be taken not to commit oneself totally to preventing the shot (unless the attacker definitely attempts to shoot), as this tends to straighten the body, lifting the centre of gravity high, and leaves the defender open to the fake shot and drive manoeuvre. Also, in this situation a defender should never jump to prevent the shot unless absolutely certain the shot is being taken – better to maintain position and deny the drive to a higher percentage shooting area.

The drive is prevented by movement of the feet. Lateral quickness is necessary to move to a new defensive position, allied with good body control and balance. If the defender is playing good positional defence, close up to the attacking player to deny the shot, the attacker will try to fake the defence out of position in order to take advantage of the situation. The defence, therefore, must know the manoeuvres available to the attacker and learn how to master the situation. The defender should be prepared to give up the outside shot on occasions in order to prevent the drive for the better inside shot.

If the attacker drives, the defender must learn how to 'steer' him away from his intended path. Generally the defender should take up a position *in line* with the attacker with the ball and the basket. By taking up this position, all outside shots have to be taken over the defence and passes to the under-basket area are discouraged, although it allows the possibility of the attacker being able to manoeuvre for a drive down either side of the defender. The latter can be somewhat reduced if the defender establishes a defensive position *off-line* between the attacker and basket. That is, the defender positions himself slightly to one side of an imaginary line drawn between the attacker and the basket. By taking up such a position, the attacker is encouraged to drive in one direction to a 'safe' area, whilst the danger side is being overplayed and, therefore, the drive discouraged down that side. By positioning the body and feet correctly, the defensive player whilst overplaying one side should be able to 'steer' the driving player down the other, possibly towards a sideline or towards his team-mates where help can be given.

Players should be discouraged from reaching for the ball, as this tends to cause contact and therefore fouls. Defenders should be encouraged to move their feet and if an attacking player drives, quickly take up a defensive position in front of the driver and take any contact which occurs on the chest, which will result in the driver being called for charging. At all times the defender should be prepared to hustle and present a challenge to the man he is guarding.

When defending an attacker away from the basket *without* the ball, many of the principles outlined earlier should still be applied, but the best defence of all is to deny him the ball. If he hasn't got the ball, obviously he can't shoot, drive or pass; but this form of defence, applied by all members of the team away from the ball whilst extreme pressure is applied on the ball, needs good individual defensive skill and is the basis of most pressing defences which are covered more fully in Chapter 7.

Before pressure defences can be applied, players must learn the basic manoeuvres of individual defence and in particular that of defence away from the ball. Where possible, defenders should position themselves to see both the ball and their defensive assignment. This is achieved by the defender sagging towards his own basket and partly turning towards the ball to make use of his peripheral vision which produces a triangle – with the ball, his attacker and himself at the three corners (see Diagram 7, player D4). The farther the attacker is away from the ball, the farther the defender can, within reason, afford to sag towards his basket to give support in depth should the player with the ball (O7) break through the defence on a drive to the basket. The closer the ball comes to his attacker, the nearer he should be, until the ball is only one pass away, when he should be in such a position as to deny or discourage the pass being made.

This form of defence can be termed an *in-line sagging defence* and can be improved upon by using an *off-line sag*. That is, instead of sagging directly in-line with the attacker and basket, move towards the ball at the same time as sagging towards the basket (see Diagram 7, player D6). Not only is the defender

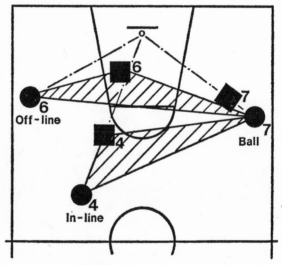

7. Defence away from the ball

now between the attacker and his own basket, but also between the attacker and the ball, which may discourage any cross-court passes, provide opportunites for intercepting the ball and also give support to D7 should O7 break free with the ball.

When defending a player about to receive a pass, slightly overplay the passing lane, watching both the ball and the attacker. This is not always possible and it may be necessary to make contact with the attacker by 'feeling' for him with the forearm whilst looking at the ball and using the other arm to discourage the pass. Care must be taken not to hold or push the attacker when making contact in this way, otherwise a foul will result. Footwork is important when defending in this situation.

When defending against a possible pass being received by an attacker from the defender's left-hand side, the defender should overplay that side with the left leg forward, half facing the attacker with the left arm flexed in such a position as to discourage the pass. The defender should have his head turned to a mid position between the receiver and passer to make use of his peripheral vision, and be continually adjusting his position to meet that of the receiver. In order to concentrate more on the ball, but at the same time maintain a good position, the defender can 'feel' for the receiver with his right forearm, which calls for a closer defensive position, and all directional movement is then felt by the defender.

PRACTICES FOR DEFENDING AWAY FROM THE BASKET

1. *Against Guards:* A queue of attacking players is formed with the head of the queue standing on the free-throw line facing the basket. A defensive player gives the ball to the first player in line and plays him 1-on-1 practising defence whilst the attacker has the option of shooting or driving. Progression is maintained by the defender joining the queue and the attacker becoming the next defender against the next player in line.

2. *Against Forwards:* Form a queue at the centre circle with an attacker and his defender in a Forward position, similar to that shown in Diagram 1. The first player in the queue passes the ball to the attacker, who has broken out to a position on the side from which he can shoot. The defender now plays him 1-on-1 and progression is by having the defender join the queue; the attacker becomes the next defender and the passer becomes the next attacking player.

Check points

* Body balance and footwork.
* Stop the shot – use of the hands.
* Stop the drive – movement of the feet.
* Stop the pass – use of hands and movement of feet.
* Positional play – in-line and off-line defence.

DEFENCE CLOSE TO THE BASKET

Potentially this is the most dangerous area to defend in. Players receiving the ball close to the basket have a higher percentage success rate in scoring, due to their nearness: in order to discuss this situation, 'close' will be considered to be in and around the free-throw area.

The free-throw area is the province of the Post players, who are usually the tallest and strongest attackers in the team, and should therefore be matched in defence with the same physical attributes where possible. At all times the ball should be discouraged or, better still, denied to players in this area, as not only are they a high scoring threat, but they can pass the ball from a central source to any other offensive position on court, thus creating scoring opportunities for their team-mates.

When defending the Post player, three basic offensive positions have to be considered. These are as follows:
(a) Post player in the high position on the free-throw line.
(b) Post player in the side position about half-way down the free-throw lane.
(c) Post player in the low position where the free-throw lane meets the baseline.

All the defensive principles mentioned earlier in this chapter still apply, and the defender should generally endeavour to overplay the passing lane between the ball and the Post player wherever the ball may be. This method of defence has already been discussed on page 51, and in this case involves the defender playing half round the Post player on the ball side to help discourage the pass being made. With rapid movement of the ball this is not always possible. As the defender transfers from one side of the Post player to the other, a decision has to be made as to whether to do this by going behind or in front of the Post. By going behind, the Post is always available in this instance to receive a pass, but is prevented from going direct to the basket and therefore has to shoot over the defensive player. By going across the front of the Post (i.e. between the ball and the Post player), this prevents the direct pass, but opens up the possibility of the Post player, stepping back towards the basket, looking for a pass over the top of the defender. This latter manoeuvre by the defence can be successfully used providing there is co-operation between all five defenders, and one or more of them have sagged to cut off the possibility of the Post player stepping backwards to the basket.

Whenever a Post player cuts across the free-throw lane or moves from the low to the high posititition looking to receive the ball, the defender should anticipate the move and try to beat him to the spot, thus denying him the position he wanted and also preventing him from receiving the ball.

It will be impossible to stop the Post player from receiving the ball the whole time, and whenever the ball is fed into the Post the defender should ensure that he is not caught out of position, thus being unable to offer any further defence. Because of the close proximity of the basket, the defender should take up a position behind the Post player (between ball and basket), who will generally have his back to the basket when receiving the ball. In this position the defender should keep his hands high to discourage the shot as the post player pivots to face the basket, and by movement of his feet should endeavour to prevent the Post from driving. Where possible the Post player should be forced to pass the ball back to the outside away from the basket.

If the Post player attempts to shoot, either from the spot or off the drive, the defender should try to block the shot, or at least make him shoot over a raised arm to ensure that good position is maintained on defence if the shot be missed. Unless the defender has superior height or jumping ability, he will have to anticipate to some extent when the Post player is going to shoot, in order to jump a little sooner and a little higher to block the shot. This is dangerous, as the defender can be faked into jumping too early, and if not timed correctly it can lead to a foul being called through striking the shooting arm and not the ball. If at a disadvantage, it is better for the defender to jump with the shooter and block out on landing.

Not all players who play close to the basket are Post players. Forwards may occasionally move into this area to receive the ball and would in this instance take on the responsibilities of a Post. All defensive players, therefore, should learn to play defence close to the basket, with the best defence of all being to deny each attacker the ball.

PRACTICES FOR DEFENDING CLOSE TO THE BASKET

1. *Guard-to-Post Defence:* A queue is formed at the centre circle with the first player in line with the ball. A Post player and defender are initially stationed at the low or side position. The defender tries to prevent the Post player receiving the ball in the high position (free-throw line area) from the first player in the queue. If the Post player receives the ball, the defender plays him 1-on-1 to the basket. Rotation is Passer to Post, Post to Defence, Defence to back of queue.

2. *Forward-to-Post Defence:* A queue is formed on the sideline free-throw line extended with the first player in line with the ball. A Post player and defender are initially stationed on the near side free-throw lane. The defender tries to prevent the Post player receiving the ball in the high, side or low position, and if unable to do so, then defends 1-on-1. Rotation as in Practice 1.

3. As in Practice 2, but have the Post player and defender stationed initially on the far side free-throw lane and have the Post manoeuvre across the free-throw lane to meet the pass.

Check points

* Good body balance and footwork.

* Discourage the pass by playing half round between ball and receiver.

* Discourage the shot – use of hands and arms.

* Discourage the drive – 'steer' away from the basket.

* Positional play – defensive adjustment after the ball has been received.

BLOCKING OUT AND REBOUNDING

No team can win without scoring and no team can score without the ball. Good rebounding is ball control. It has been said that 'whichever team controls the boards will win the game', and this is relatively true if the following example is considered. Assuming two opposing teams are having the same percentage success on shots taken, with all other aspects of the game being equal, it can therefore be seen that whichever team takes the most shots will win the game. In order to take more shots, a team needs possession of the ball more often, and one way of achieving this is to secure the ball on each occasion of a missed shot through better rebounding. Obviously it would not be possible to obtain possession on every missed shot occasion, particularly at both the offensive and defensive ends of the court, but through correct positional play and good rebounding, the odds could be tilted in a team's favour.

Rebounding favours the defensive team, for as the shot is taken they are usually already positioned between the attacker and the basket, around which the ball will rebound should the shot be missed. If the attacking team is at a disadvantage when rebounding on offence, it should endeavour to raise its shooting percentage, therefore offering fewer rebounds to the opposition. Conversely, the defence should make the opposition miss more shots, therefore providing more opportunities for possession without being scored against.

Height is an important factor in rebounding and the closer a player is to the basket, the better his chances are of getting the ball. Timing and jumping ability are equally important, as height is of little value unless a player knows how to use it and when to use it.

As a shot is taken, it is the defensive rebounder's mission to take up a good position and block out. 'Blocking out' is the term used when a defender takes up a position between the opposing rebounder and the basket, and legally prevents him from going to the basket for the rebound. This 'inside' position is most desirable, as the player on the 'outside' must either rebound over the top of the defender or hope the ball bounces over and out of the reach of the defender. It is also important that the defender blocking out, in his keenness to obtain the inside position, does not get himself too far under the basket, otherwise the ball will rebound over the top of him and his inside position will then be at a disadvantage.

At the precise moment of the shot being taken, the actual rebound should be of secondary importance with blocking out being the priority. If all five defenders in this situation performed this manoeuvre successfully, the defence would *always* get the ball!

The action of blocking out is firstly to watch the attacker to see which direction he will take towards the basket in trying to secure the rebound. As the attacker makes his move, the defender should pivot into his intended path and 'steer' him in the direction of his movement to ensure that he himself maintains the inside position. Pivoting into the path of an opponent is performed by stepping in a forward motion towards the attacker (front pivot), or by stepping in a backward movement (rear pivot), in each case to present the defender's back as an obstacle between the attacker and the rebound. The defender may not hold or push in any way to accomplish this, and by the same token the attacker may not pull or push against the defender. Once in the under-basket rebound area, the defender should hold his ground and keep the attacker on his back. Where possible it would be better to keep the attacker away from the rebound area, by steering and blocking out much farther from the basket, thus not allowing the attacker to manoeuvre for a closer position. In this way a tall attacker no longer has the advantage over a small defender.

If players are in close proximity to the basket when the shot is taken, the defenders will not necessarily have time to watch for the attackers' movements before blocking out. In such a situation the defenders should immediately pivot and take up a position on the inside, 'feeling' for any lateral movement by the attackers through the contact with their backs.

Once in the rebound position, the rebounder should be on balance with his feet spread and knees bent to provide a strong base from which to jump, and also to prevent being pushed around by the attacker. The head should be erect and eyes focused on the ball. The arms need to be flexed at the elbows with the hands in a raised position. In this position the upper arms can also be used to 'feel' for any lateral movement of the attacker even though he cannot be seen, and they are in a state of readiness to grab the rebound.

When leaping for the rebound, timing is important. Through practice and experience, the rebounder will be able to judge the rebound from the flight of the ball in the air and should ideally time his jump to secure the ball at the highest point of his leap. The ball should be caught firmly, preferably with both hands and snatched out of the air, offering protection with the body and elbows. On landing, the ball should be protected and immediately got away from the congested under-basket area by a pass to a team-mate. If this is not possible, it should be dribbled to a safe area before a pass is made.

Rebounders should keep after the ball whilst it is in the air. Rebounds are not always taken cleanly the first time, but the second or third attempt may secure the ball for the defence.

PRACTICES FOR BLOCKING OUT AND REBOUNDING
1. All the defensive practices discussed earlier may be adjusted to include blocking out and rebounding after the shot has been taken in the 1-on-1 situation.
2. Have four pairs of attackers and defenders position themselves at about 5 metres from the basket. Get one attacker to take an outside shot (the defender to allow this) and all defenders block out before rebounding. The attackers should be allowed to pass the ball to provide different shooting angles, but are not allowed to roam freely before the shot. Progression is by feeding a different pair in from one side after each rebound attempt, whilst the pair on the far side drops out and joins the queue. In this way each pair has four attempts from four different positions on court before dropping out and changing round.
3. As for Practice 2, but let a game be played 4-on-4. Progression is the same, but whichever team gets the rebound plays on offence for the next attempt.

Check points

* Locate the attacker and block out.
* 'Feel' with the back and upper arms, and 'steer' the attacker.
* Body balance and footwork.
* Agility and timing of the rebound.
* Secure the ball firmly with both hands.
* Protect the ball with the body and elbows.

4. Pre-tactical Skills — Offence

When an attacking player is stopped in the 1-on-1 situation the value of the other players in the team comes to light. Players who stand around waiting for the ball or who just run anywhere are of little value. If all four players were to stand waiting for the ball there would be no progress, and if they were to run freely then there would be chaos.

To obtain order, whilst at the same time allowing movement, certain restrictions have to be applied, but this does not mean that players will be regimented in their movement, for if this happened the offensive pattern would be predictable and therefore easier to defend against. Order is created by establishing 'links' between players, and the first form of link is between those players who are involved with the ball. When a player is stopped and he passes the ball a link is established. Utilising this link to increase the offensive manoeuvres is the basis upon which team offence is built. The two-man plays, for that is what the links are called, require certain actions to be performed by each player, and it is vital that good grounding in 'Individual Offence' is obtained before any of the two-man plays are attempted. A number of two-man plays are shown in Diagram 8.

THE WALL PASS

The first play, which is most effective for beginners, is the wall pass. It is similar in nature to the wall pass used in every other team game except rugby.

The player who has gone through the shoot, drive, pass

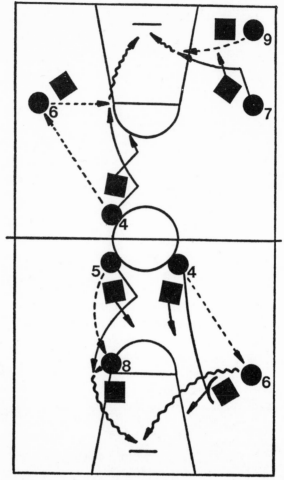

8. Two-man plays

sequence and finds himself only able to pass, cuts to the basket
after passing, looking for the return pass as he does so. Whilst
this is happening the other players will stay out of the way, but
should the return pass prove impossible, further 'links' are
established immediately. The movement of the players and the
ball is shown in the top left-hand corner of Diagram 8, but a
more detailed explanation is :

ACTION

Player O4   Player O6
  Shoot
  Drive   Get Free
  Pass — — — — — — —→ Receive
                                         Shoot
  Cut to Basket   Drive
  Receive ←— — — return — —Pass
  Shoot
  Drive – Shot

CUTTING TO THE BASKET

When a player passes the ball to a team-mate he should start his initial movement away from the direction of the pass, and if the defender is watching the ball he continues his run straight to the basket (top half of Diagram 9).

If the defender is watching the passer then the passer should check his movement, change direction, and cut to the basket on the ball side of his defender, signalling for the ball as he does so. His team-mate (O6) on receiving the ball should look for his shot and his drive in order to stop the defender sagging. The return pass will generally be a two-handed overhead pass and is critical in its timing. If it is made too early then the defence can sag off and help out against the cutting player. If it is made too late the cutting player will have his back to the ball or will be running sideways not looking where he is going. One common fault with players cutting to the basket is that they stop and wait for the ball. If a player is stationary he is the easiest player to defend against and not only that, he is usually blocking up the middle also. It is important, therefore, that players, who cut to the basket on 2-on-2 situations, continue their cut all the way to the basket and out to the opposite corner when they do not receive the return pass. A 2-on-2 play is finished when the return pass is made, or the cutting player has gone past the angle of return pass without receiving it, but from this point further links are established with other players. In fact, offensive basketball is a continuous set of two-man plays. The wall pass

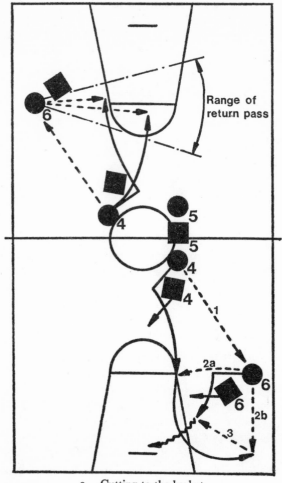

Range of
return pass

9.   Cutting to the basket

is the simplest of these and adequate for team tactics for the less
experienced players.

1. Initially the players should be given the opportunity of learning the concept of the wall pass before efforts are made to teach
the finer points. This can be done best in game form, and

Method 2 of 'introducing the game' is a suitable organisation. The game should be conditioned and include a futher 'Teachers' Rule' – 'Pass and cut to the basket every time, wherever you are on court.'

NOTE: Coaches and teachers should insist that when a player passes he cuts to the basket, looking for a return pass. The player should run *under* the basket and go out to the opposite corner, i.e. if the pass was made to the right when he faced the basket, he cuts and goes out to the left-hand corner. Similarly if he passes to the left, he cuts to the basket and then goes to the right-hand corner. The rule should be strictly enforced even for a player who passes from the corner 'outwards'. He will in fact cut to the basket and come back to the same position.

Once the concept of pass, cut, signal for return pass has been grasped within a game, the finer points can be coached in a more isolated game situation. Care should be taken to help the players to realise that it is an organised form of getting a man free for a shot.

2. *To condition the timing of the return pass:* The practice is similar to the one for 'Getting Free to Receive', except that the Guard-to-Forward situation is conditioned to have the Guard cut to the basket and the defender marks the Forward.

3. *To pressurise the cutting players in getting past the Defender:* This practice is as the previous one, but the defender marks the player in the Guard position who cuts to the basket.

The rotation for both practices is Guard to Forward, Forward to Defender, Defender behind the queue.

4. *The whole 2-on-2 situation:* For large groups it is suggested that the court is divided into quarters as for some of the previous practices and each group keep to its own quarter in the first instance. In each quarter there would be a 2-on-2 situation of Guard-to-Forward and another one or two pairs in the queue. The movement of the players is as shown in the bottom half of Diagram 9. If the player O4 is not free to receive the return pass 2a when cutting for the basket, he should go to the corner (in this case only, the same side as the ball) and thus a new 2-on-2 situation can start immediately with the pass 2b. This organisa-

tion gives more than one opportunity of practising the wall pass within the one-game situation.

The rotation is for O4 and D4 to take O6's and D6's place and the ball starts at the starting-point again at the front of the queue. O6 and D6 got to the back of the queue. It will help with the smooth running of the practice if the attacker is the same in each pair at the Guard and Forward positions. They can change over every time they rejoin the queue. Similar practices can go on in each quarter of the court all at the same time. The starting position for each action is with the attacker standing on the centre circle and his team colleague level with the free-throw line about 2 metres away from it.

5. To make sure that the players have equal opportunity of practising on each side of the court, players who are due to rejoin the queue should join the queue in the next quarter of the court going in a clockwise direction. In this case the attacker in each pair will remain the attacker until one circuit of the court is completed.

THE WALL PASS USED BY THE FORWARD AND CORNER PLAYER

A slight variation of the wall pass can be introduced into Practice 4. It would take place if the first return pass was unable to be made and the Guard cut to the basket and then the corner. The Forward, after passing to the corner player, would run towards the corner and cut behind his own defender straight to the basket. This option is illustrated in the top right-hand corner of Diagram 8. It is a particularly useful option if the defender is playing between the man and the ball instead of the man and basket.

The Post Play

This is the second 2-on-2 play and care should be taken not to introduce it too early in a player's experience, for it requires knowledge of the concept of 'no contact', whilst at the same time making full use of legal obstruction. The coach therefore has a problem, but he can get over this by full understanding of the rules and their interpretations.

1. Palma (7) of Mexico jump shooting over the straight arm defence of Christov (Bulgaria)

2. Rullan (Spain) jump shooting over the tight defence of a Greek player. Note No. 7 of Greece preparing to block out

3. *Above left:* G. Anderson (4) shows follow through during execution of right hand jump shot in an England v. Portugal match

4. *Above right:* A. Warner demonstrates good technique of left handed lay-up shot. England v. Portugal

5. *Left:* Good timing secures offensive rebound for K. Godwin. England v. Portugal

The Post play is a 2-on-2 play which generally takes place between a player who plays on the 'outside', i.e. Guard or Forward, and a player who plays on the 'inside', i.e. Post player, who generally plays with his back to the basket.

Specialisation should not be started too early, but during this stage of the players' development certain individuals may have a preference for playing close to the basket or with their back to it. They are usually the tall ones, but they should also realise that they cannot afford to forget how to play outside as well, for when they get into higher levels of basketball they may not be tall enough to play 'the Post.' Also it is just as important that all players master the basic skills of playing with their backs to the basket.

The actions of a 2-on-2 post play are shown in the bottom left corner of Diagram 8. Player O5, again unable to shoot or drive, passes the ball to the Post player O8, who receives it with his back to the basket. O5 then cuts to the basket, steering his defender D5 into O8. Player O8 in the meantime has turned as far round as he can in order to face the basket. Consequently, D5 is steered into the back or side of O8 At that moment in time O5 and O8 only have one defender (D8) between them and the basket. Whichever attacker is free – usually O5 – takes the ball and drives for the basket. If the defender switches to O5, then O8 can shoot or drive. The success of the action depends upon whether O5 is able to steer his defender D5 into 'the Post', namely O8, in order to get himself free.

Practices for this activity should follow clearly defined lines so that the learner only has to learn one thing at a time, and gets a shot as a reward for success.

PRACTICE TO TEACH THE ATTACKER HOW TO STEER HIS DEFENDER INTO A STATIONARY OBJECT

1. The object used may be a rolled-up agility mattress placed on its end at the edge of the free-throw line to represent a Post player. A Guard together with a defender are stationed at the centre circle and a Forward is positioned near the sideline, free-throw line extended nearest the mattress. The Guard passes the

C

ball to the Forward and runs his defender into the mattress, which is being held upright by the Forward's defender. As the Guard loses his defender, he receives a return pass and goes on to shoot. The guard rebounds his own shot and passes the ball to the next pair in the queue. The Forward and his 'defender' (mattress holder) join the queue, whilst the Guard becomes the next Forward and his defender holds up the mattress. Each pair stays together and they change over responsibilities each time they perform the pass and cut manoeuvre. This activity can be practised in each quarter of the court as in previous practices.

Check points

* Pause after passing.
* Watch the defender's movement.
* Don't make too many changes of direction.
* Make sure the defender hits the *mattress*.

2. *To teach the post player the movements of his position:* The same practice, but dispense with the mattress. The player who should be holding it up now becomes the object. He should stand on the corner of the free-throw line facing the attacking Guard, and turn to face the basket when the pass is made to the Forward. When turning to face the basket, he should turn round by stepping forward and round with the inside foot (foot nearest the centre of court) and using the outside foot as the pivot foot. He steps forward with the inside foot because in the game he will be closely defended and unable to pivot backwards in order to face the basket. When he has the ball in a later practice, he will also be keeping it away from his close defender.

Check points

* Land on the free-throw line with both feet at the same time.
* When the Guard passes the ball, pivot forwards and round to face the basket.
* Brace yourself for the bump.

3. A 2-on-1 situation is used. It is as shown in the bottom left-hand corner of Diagram 8, but on this occasion, the Post player's defender is omitted. The actions are as described for that of the Post play. The Post player is not allowed to drive for the basket when he turns to face it. When the Guard goes past the Post he should be given the ball if he is free. If he is

not free, the Post player should be given the opportunity of shooting. Rotation is Guard to Defender, Defender to Post, Post behind the queue.

4. The full 2-on-2 Guard-to-Post situation with no switching of defenders. It is made rotational by working in pairs, and each pair goes to Guard, to Post, to the queue and then changes over.

At this stage each attacking player has further things to do if the defender decides to switch responsibilities half-way through the action. When the attacking Guard runs his defender into the Post player and runs on through, the Post player's defender may switch and pick up the Guard as soon as he gets the ball. The Post player must then cut directly towards the basket at this instance to receive a pass back from the Guard, for he will be free to do so since the other defender will be behind him. This action is known as rolling to the basket.

5. Full 2-on-2 situation with defenders allowed to switch.

Check points for the guard

* Pass to the Post player.
* Run the defender into the Post.
* Receive the ball.
* Return the pass if the defender switches.

Check points for the post player

* Receive the pass.
* Pivot forwards and outwards to face the basket.
* Return the pass.
* Cut to the basket.
* Keep an eye on the ball ready for a further return pass.

6. A full game with a 'Teachers' Rule' to condition the game. This rule is 'pass and go behind the player you pass to'. This action will result in many Post play actions happening all over the court. Failure to 'go behind' results in that team being called for a violation of the 'Teachers' Rule'.

THE SCREEN PLAY

The third 2-on-2 play, which is the most complicated of the two-man plays, is the 'Screen play'. It involves a player making a pass and then setting a screen for that player to drive to the basket, at the same time losing his defender by running the defender into the screen (see the bottom right-hand corner of Diagram 8). Many teachers try this before the post play, but this should be discouraged for the attacking player is expected to run his defender into the screen whilst dribbling. In the post play he learns to run his defender into a blockage without dribbling, thus making the screen play an obvious progression from the post play. The action requires player O4 to pass the ball to O6 and set the screen, i.e. to stand still at a point slightly behind and to the side of O6's defender. Player O6 then dribbles to the basket, steering his defender into the screen. At this point, as in the post play, two attackers face one defender. The one who is free takes the ball and drives for the basket. The roll to the basket is also included. The moment the screen is effective, the actions are similar to the post play.

SETTING SCREENS

The rules for setting a screen are quite specific and also apply to the Post player, for he acts as a screen during the action of a post play. Screens that can be seen by the opponent may be set at any distance away from the opponent, short of actual contact. Screens that are blind, that is, unable to be seen by the opponents, must be set at least one metre away from the opponent. The screener may face in any direction. Once the screen has been set, the screener may not move except in the same direction and path as his opponent.

PRACTICES FOR THE PASS AND SCREEN

1. The practice is organised in a 2-on-1 situation with a Guard and a Forward who is defended. The Guard should pass the ball to the Forward and set the screen on the defender of the Forward. The Forward runs his defender into the screen and drives for the basket. The practice is made rotational by the defender throwing the ball to the front of the queue after he has retrieved the shot, and the others move round in the usual order at the moment the shot is taken, viz. Guard to Forward, Forward to Defender, Defender behind the queue. Again, for a

class activity, the practice can be done in the four quarters of the court.

Check points for the player setting the screen

* Stand still and in the proposed path of the defender.
* After the screen is effective roll to the basket, facing the ball at all times.

Check points for the player using the screen

* Use a foot fake away from the screen to start the drive.
* Drive close to the screen.

2. In pairs using a full 2-on-2 situation and utilising the Guard and Forward positions. Defenders are not allowed to switch.

3. As previous practice but with defenders being allowed to switch.

4. A full game conditioned by a 'Teachers' Rule' of 'Pass and Screen'. The violation of this rule results in possession for the opposing team.

The Relationship of Positions

At the beginning of the book there is a diagram of the attacking positions (page 14). This is to enable the reader to understand more fully the text in the first few chapters, and to become familiarised with the worldwide terminology used in the game. It is important to note that the names are given to the offensive positions on court, not to individuals, although very often these names are used in connection with players. Players in the team will have some identifying talents which will cause them to play in particular positions more than in others, and so they get the tag of being a Guard, or Forward, or Post player.

The GUARD is the ball-carrier in the team and generally the instigator of any team offensive manoeuvres. Because of the demands of the position he will usually be good at passing the ball, and be a good analyst in terms of deciding which tactics to use for pentrating the defence. He will have to be a good dribbler of the ball if he is the carrier, and being able to dribble with both hands will increase his ability to set the team offensive machine in motion. Since he plays outside the defensive framework he will be expected to shoot well from the 'outside', and since all players will be martialled between him and the offensive goal, he will be required to act as 'spoiler' of any quick offensive manoeuvres by the opposition resulting from a change of possession. He will also have to get free to receive passes from his own team-mates should they be in trouble, this function being generally known as 'Safety Man'.

The FORWARD is the term used for the player who plays down the sides of the court. The function of the Forward is multiple. Working alone from that position demands a good outside shot and the agility to be able to drive into the middle and score, but the Forward should also be prepared to link with all other players. His tactical brain will be called upon too in this respect, for if the play is down the other side of the court, the weak side Forward has to decide whether to go and act as safety man or to cut into the gaps in the middle. With his linking activities, the Forward may well be found in any position on the court, which suggests he is usually the all-round player.

The POST position is the area close to the basket, and obviously height is a considerable advantage. A player playing in the Post uses his height in three different ways. Firstly, passes into that position from players linking with the Post are easier to make to and from the high position, due to the congestion in that area. Secondly, his height will enable him to take clearer shots against opponents, and if close to the basket he will be able to take shots which are so much nearer to the basket and therefore more difficult to intercept (lay-up), and thirdly, he will be able to use his height to challenge effectively for rebounds when his team-mates have failed to score.

Having identified the individual characteristics of each playing position, it is necessary to see how these can be linked together to utilise the two-man plays. The two-man plays, it will be remembered, are the wall pass, the post play, and the screen play. The links that are established must have fluency and also be practicable on the court of play. They must also be easy to identify, for in the team play the players not involved should remember that they have their part to play in the success of any two-man plays by keeping out of the way, at the same time as keeping their defenders out of the way. The relationships which are established must apply equally to each side of the court. The recognisable cue for the establishment of a relationship or link is the passing of the ball between two players. The basic relationships between Guard and Forward, and Guard and Post are detailed in the earlier parts of this chapter.

When building a team play, not all of the possibilities will be used of course, but it will help the coach in deciding which ones to use if he bears in mind the ability of his players and the flair that they have for particular actions. It should not be forgotten that the relationships which are developed are for the purpose of creating a scoring opportunity and the individual options still apply, although there may be a slight change of emphasis.

Since the relationships are part and parcel of team play, they can be used as specific practices to overcome certain inadequacies, and any particular part of the team play which needs attention can be practiced in isolation in game form.

There are other practices which can be used to develop specific items for the whole team. These practices are conditioned games where all five attacking players accept the condition.

PRACTICES

1. A half-court game practice for the wall pass. A horseshoe formation in the attacking half of the court is used and the ball starts with the Guard. By passing the ball, cutting to the basket, circulating out to the opposite side with everyone moving round to fill the positions left free, a very useful continuous practice is obtained. The object of the practice is to make a clear return pass to the cutter for an attempt at scoring. If this is not possible, the process continues until it is.

2. A half-court game practice for the screen play. A similar organisation to the previous activity, but each player passes, screens and rolls to the basket.

3. A 3-on-3 game in one quarter of the court to develop the relationship between Guard, Forward and Post.

However, these actions can be extended to take part in other situations when a link is established. Wall passes and post plays can be performed between Forward and Post, two Forwards on the same side of the court, and Post and baseline Forward positions.

With the inclusion of a third player, combinations of wall passes and post plays can be obtained between Guards, Forwards and Posts, creating opportunities for a succession of two-man plays, should the initial attempt to use 'a link' not create a scoring opportunity. Such combinations can use the movement of the wall pass or post play without the ball, whilst the ball is in the possession of the third player, making at least one player free to receive the ball for a shot.

These movements are built up by players perfecting the actions of two-man plays and being able to time their movements to coincide with the actions and movements of the other players so that a fluent sequence of events takes place.

An example of such an action between the Guard, Forward and Post is as follows :

The Guard passes to the Post and moves according to a post play action. The Forward on that side of the court, seeing that the Post player is unable to turn to the basket, also moves to make a post play action with the Post player, timing his movements to pass the Post player just after the Guard.

The Post player on this occasion is able to make a short 'give' pass to either the Guard or the Forward. This action involving three players is generally known as 'Splitting the Post'. This manoeuvre can be performed also by two Forwards and the Post on the same side of the court.

Another example of a combination play resulting from the relationship between two Forwards and the Post is when a Forward passes to another Forward in the corner on the same side, and cuts to the basket for a return pass. The Post player on the free-throw line times his cut to the basket to follow in behind the first cutting player, as if the Post player himself had passed the ball to the corner. The Forward in the corner would then have an alternative return pass should the first one be blocked.

5. *Pre-tactical Skills — Defence*

We have already stated in offence that links between players, upon which a team offence can be built, are necessary. This is also true when considering defence. Individual defence must be related to the 'whole' and when performed collectively is the basis for team defence.

As team offence is built up of two- and three-man plays, the individual defenders must develop an understanding of these basic manoeuvres and learn how to combat them with the additional aid of their own team-mates.

One of the greatest aids at the disposal of the defence is that of *communication*. Players should be continually informing their team-mates of any danger developing or where adjustments are needed to provide for a more solid defence. Use of the voice is the most important means of communication in defence, especially when offensive manoeuvres such as screens are being set on the 'blind' side of players busily concentrating on the man with the ball. In situations such as this 'screen left' or 'screen right' may be shouted by the screener's defender, in order that the defender being screened is aware of the fact and can take measures to avoid or fight around the screen. When an attacker breaks through on a drive, 'help' should be communicated to the defenders nearer the basket. In fact, whenever an adjustment is needed in defence, communication is necessary, whether it be by use of words, hand signals or by physical contact between team-mates.

Defence With the Help of Team-Mates

The next step from the 1-on-1 defence covered in Chapter 3 involves additional players, as the attacking team develops its two- and three-man plays.

Within the development of two-man plays, the offence can create situations of divergence and convergence. The former can be the use of pass and cut plays (i.e. the 'wall pass'), which retains the element of individual defence (see the top half of Diagram 8). That is, 1-on-1 defence on the player WITH the ball defending the shot, drive, pass procedures, and on the player WITHOUT the ball, discouraging or denying the return pass as he goes to the basket. The latter situation that of convergence, occurs when the main area of help is required to defend against the pass and follow procedures and screen play situations (see the bottom half of Diagram 8).

Further defensive principles must be understood and learnt when defending against convergent plays in the 2-on-2 situation; these being to 'stick', and how and when to 'slide' and 'switch' as screen plays develop.

Sticking Defence

This is the ability to 'stick' with an attacker and not allow oneself to get screened off, but to fight over and through screens. This is perhaps the best defence of all, as it enables the defender to play against the same attacker throughout, without any mis-matches occurring through having to switch. In this way, the coach is able to match the attributes of an attacker with those of a specific defender, but it is a demanding role to play, requires good defensive techniques and a sound communication link between players.

Convergent 2-on-2 plays can develop 'on' the ball or 'away' from the ball. Plays involving the ball are most critical to the defence, as a mistake in this situation can result in a basket being scored.

When defending an attacker cutting towards a Post player who has the ball, looking for a give pass (top left-hand corner of Diagram 10), the defender (D4) should slightly overplay the

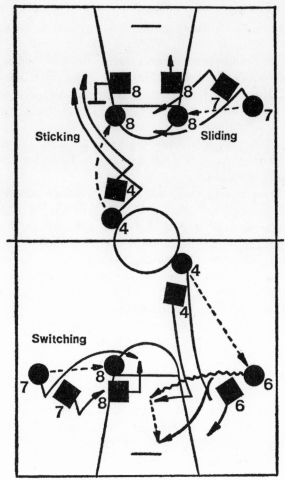

10. Defence with the help of team-mates

attacker's direction of movement. This forces the attacker to swing wide of the Post and therefore allows room for the defender to squeeze through between the ball and his attacker and thus 'stick' with his defensive assignment. Care must be taken by D4 not to overplay the attacker too much, otherwise a quick change of direction may find D4 screened off as the attacker cuts by the other side of the Post.

The player defending the Post with the ball towards whom an attacker is advancing, should 'inform' D4 of the developments and help out where necessary. At this point, the player defending the cutter is concentrating on his man and is 'blind' to the screen developing behind him – communication in this situation, therefore, is the responsibility of the Post player's defender (D8). Help can be given by D8 by overplaying the side down which the attacker is cutting. This also forces the cutter to swing slightly wide of the Post, thus allowing the cutter's defender to 'stick' with his assignment and prevent him from receiving the pass.

A similar situation develops when, instead of passing to the Post and cutting, the Guard drives towards the Post, trying to lose his defender on the stationary screen set by the Post. The defence should react in the same way described earlier, with the Guard's defender overplaying the dribble and steering the Guard away from the screen where possible, whilst the Post's defender overplays the Post on the same side as the driving player, forcing the Guard to swing slightly wide to allow the defender to 'stick' with his man. If the Post's defender can force the dribbler to stop and pick up the ball, even better.

SLIDING DEFENCE

This manoeuvre is used when the defender is unable to 'stick' with his attacker by fighting over the top as a screen play develops (top right-hand corner of Diagram 10). In order to maintain contact with his defensive assignment, player D7 'slides' through between O8 and D8 as O7 passes the ball and cuts over the top of O8, using the Post as a screen. This again requires communication between the defensive players, for when O8 receives the ball, D8 will automatically close up to defend against the possible shot and therefore provide an even larger obstacle (two players) in the path of D7. Player D8 would see the play developing and should inform D7 of the possible screen. If D7 is unable to go over the top with O7, D8 should step back to provide a gap through which D7 can 'slide' and again pick up O7 as he moves round the Post. The danger area of this manoeuvre is when the actual 'slide' takes place, as no one at this precise moment is defending O7. If he should stop and receive the ball back from O8, he has an unopposed shot at the basket with the defenders trying to adjust their positions behind the Post.

SWITCHING DEFENCE

The danger of the previous situtation can be somewhat alleviated if the defender's 'switch' assignments as a screen occurs (bottom left-hand corner of Diagram 10), but this may also lead to further dangers and complications. When it is seen that D7 is unable to stay with O7 and is about to be screen off, D8 should call 'switch' and quickly pick up O7 as he moves round the Post. D7 would then change assignments and be responsible for defending O8. To cut down the shooting possibilities of O7 as he moves over the Post, D8 may time his move to jump into the path of O7, thus preventing him from moving in the direction he wanted to and also denying the possible shot. This manoeuvre is called the JUMP SWITCH, with the defender taking up a defensive position legally in the path of an attacking player, and it is also very effective against a dribbling player.

Switching may cause a mis-match, either in height or ability, which should be avoided where possible. If it is necessary to switch, defenders should switch back to their own assignments at the earliest possible opportunity.

Switching also invariably puts one of the defenders at a disadvantage, as shown in the bottom right-hand corner of Diagram 10. After passing the ball to the Forward, player O4 sets a screen on D6. The Forward accepts the screen and drives for the basket, running D6 into the legal block. In this situation, D4 would have to 'switch' on to the Forward to prevent him going to the basket, whilst D6 picked up the Guard. If the Guard (O4) immediately rolls to the basket as the screen is accepted, looking for a return pass, D6 will find himself behind the attacker, or at least in an outside position in relation to the basket. In order to help to prevent this manoeuvre, D4 should initially inform D6 of the possible screen as the Guard follows his pass (he may shout "screen left"). Player D6 should then 'feel' for the screen being set whilst still concentrating on the player with the ball. In this way, D6 will know where the screen is and should try to go 'over the top' (i.e. stick) if the Forward accepts it. Player D4 will have moved with the Guard, and if D6 is screened off he should immediately 'jump switch' on to the Forward, endeavouring to make him pick up his dribble, and at the same time communicating this fact by calling out 'switch'.

Player D6, on finding himself screened off and hearing the 'switch' call, should quickly adjust his position and try to prevent O4 getting on the inside. This can be achieved by quickly stepping back towards the basket as the driver sets off, or by rolling off the screener to gain the inside position. The latter manoeuvre is similar to that of the offensive roll, which would be used by the screener, but in order to gain the advantage it has to be performed slightly before the attacker's move.

PRACTICES FOR PRE-TACTICAL DEFENSIVE SKILLS
These may be the same as for the Offensive Pre-Tactical Skills, but performed with a defensive bias. When players become more proficient, the offence may be practised with full defence to give a true game situation when practising 2-on-2 plays.
Check points
* Communication – vocal, visual, physical.
* Good individual technique.
* 'Fight over the top' – tight defence.
* 'Slide' when away from the ball, but never close to the basket when involving the ball.
* 'Switch' when screened off.
* 'Jump Switch' and defensive roll by team-mate.

6. Tactical Skills — Offence

THE FAST-BREAK ATTACK

The first form of attack by any team should be the FAST BREAK. Only when this is halted or when there is no possible opportunity to fast break, should a team consider moving into a form of 'half-court' offence. The fast break is fun to play and entertaining to watch, but requires extremely good physical conditioning on the part of the players and a high degree of individual and team defensive skill. Players must be taught to react immediately on the change of possession from defence to offence – 'instant offensive obedience'.

At every possible opportunity, teams should put pressure on their opponents defence by getting the ball down court and attempting to score as fast as possible. The speed in which the ball is advanced down court must be organised and controlled. The fast break starts on the change in possession at rebounds, interceptions, stolen balls, and any other opportunity when ball possession is rapidly gained.

The execution of the fast break generally occurs in one of the following four ways :

(a) *Single Man Break* – usually when an interception or stolen ball occurs in the front line on defence, resulting in a quick dribble down court for the lay-up.

(b) *2-on-1 Break* – again, usually occurs when possession is gained in the front line on defence, or from a quick outlet pass after a rebound with two players breaking free down the court with only one defensive player attempting to stop the break.

(c) *3-on-2 Break* – occurs when three players break down the court in an organised manner with two opponents attempting to stop or delay the break.

(d) *3-on-3 Break with Trailers* – usually occurs as in (c), but with three opponents managing to get back in defence.

The trailers are the other two offensive players who follow up the initial wave of attack with the possibility of going to the basket before the defence can get organised.

The organisation and control of the fast break can be broken down into four phases for proper execution.

1. BALL POSSESSION

Obviously, possession of the ball is of the utmost importance if the fast break is to function successfully, and players should be taught how possession can best be gained. Defensive rebounding is the most common way in which the ball may be obtained, and as a shot is taken players should first locate their nearest opponent, block him out legally from the boards, and then go and get the ball (see page 55).

Other ball possessions include interceptions, stolen balls, violations and following a basket by the opponents, but one of the most important features of the break at this stage is the recognition of the change of possession – the immediate transition from defence to offence.

2. OUTLET PASS

For a well-balanced controlled fast break to operate well, the speed with which the ball is transferred from the under-basket area (which is usually congested with players rebounding) to an outlet position is of the utmost importance, for the fast break is made or lost in this manoeuvre.

As soon as a shot goes up and it becomes evident that the defence will gain control of the ball, two players farthest from the ball should, after first blocking out their men, break for the outlet zones (Diagram 11). These players may be in the corners or at any other location on court, but if the ball does not rebound to either of them, they should go to the nearest outlet zone. This is very important, since as the rebounders gain control and look for a pass out they must have a target to hit.

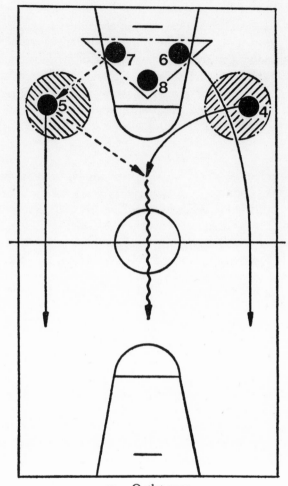

11. Outlet pass

As the players station themselves at the outlet zones and the rebound is gained, the ball should be delivered to the same side of court on which the rebound is obtained, thus eliminating any cross-court pass which might be intercepted. The outlet pass is the most important pass in the break. It is the first pass and is often delivered under considerable stress, as teams will put pressure on the rebounder to prevent a quick outlet pass. The two-hand overhead and one-hand javelin passes are probably the best to use in getting the ball to the outlet zone. Because of the difficulties that arise, the players who fill the outlet zones should provide a fairly stationary target or go to meet the ball and not start down court too soon.

An exception to the outlet pass may occur when a long rebound is obtained and the player bursts out of defence on the dribble, creating good 2-on-1 or 3-on-2 situations.

3. MOVEMENT DOWN THE COURT

The movement of players down court should be organised with three prongs of attack – one player in each of the outer lanes and the third going down the middle area. The three lanes of attack should be about 5 metres apart, which prevents any one opponent from defending two attackers.

The ball may be advanced down any lane, but once in the front court it should preferably be transferred to the middle lane as this provides more available options at the finishing end of the break.

As the rebound is obtained by player O7 in this case (Diagram 11), he passes the ball to the nearest outlet zone, and player O4 on the opposite side of the floor recognises this and prepares to break to the middle lane. He should restrain himself from going too far and thus 'running away' from this second pass. Player O5, who passes the ball to the middle, fills one lane on the break and a third player, O6 in this case, opposite the side on which the outlet pass was made, breaks at top speed to fill the other lane, whilst player O4 dribbles the ball down the middle lane.

Note that there is no passing once the ball is in the middle lane, as each pass creates a chance of error and the ball in the hands of the dribbler will probably be ahead of the cutters filling the outside lanes. If, on the other hand, a player is ahead of the dribbler, the ball should always be advanced as it can always be returned as the defence is drawn.

It may not always be possible to pass immediately to the middle lane, in which case player O5 should dribble down the outer lane and transfer the ball to the middle at the first opportunity. Alternatively, as player O5 receives the outlet pass he may himself elect to take the middle lane, in which case player O4 veers back to the outer lane, and player O8 may then fill the third lane.

In the case of possession being gained on a long rebound, the player with the ball may have the opportunity of breaking out on the dribble, with players O4 and O5 filling the outer lanes.

4. FINISHING THE BREAK

(a) *2-on-1 Situation:* In this situation the two players should again space themselves about 5 metres apart as they move down court, with neither player being in the middle lane. Here again excessive passing between them should be avoided, except when one player is in considerable advance of the other. As the free-throw area is approached, the dribbler should attempt to make the defensive player commit on him, and then deliver an open pass to his team-mate (Diagram 12). Obviously, if the defensive

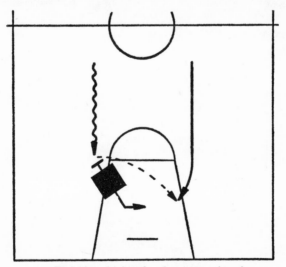

12.   Finishing the break: the 2-on-1 situation

player anticipates this and tries to cover the open man, the dribbler should drive all the way to the basket or stop off and jump shoot, whilst his team-mate goes to rebound.

A further situation which often occurs is when the dribbler is out on his own, confronted by a defensive player, but being backed up by a team-mate following down court to complete the 2-on-1 set-up. The dribbler, instead of trying to take his man 1-on-1, should stop around the free-throw line area and continue TO FACE THE BASKET. His team-mate, advancing down court from behind, should then inform him on which side he intends to make his cut by calling 'ball left' or 'ball right'.

If the defensive player remains with the ball-hander, the ball should be passed to the cutter for a lay-up, or if he sags off to pick up the cutter it leaves the ball-handler with an easy middle distance shot (free throw!).

(b) *3-on-2 Situation:* In this situation it is imperative that the dribbler (middle man) stops at the free-throw line, unless the two defensive players are split, leaving an unhampered drive to the basket. By stopping, the ball-handler can best force the defence to commit itself on him and one of the cutters moving down court (Diagram 13). By staying on the free-throw line, he also presents a good target for the cutters to feed the ball back to him if the defence are able to recover.

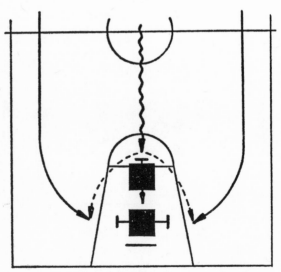

13. Finishing the break: the 3-on-2 situation

If the cutter receiving the ball is picked up by the defence, he may pass the ball on across the lane to the other cutter, but this pass is very risky and should only be thrown when there is no chance of interception.

(c) *Second Wave of Attack:* The two offensive players not involved in the three lanes of attack (usually these are the two who do the bulk of the defensive rebounding), should 'trail' the fast break down court. The quickest one down court becomes the 1st Trailer, the next one being the 2nd Trailer. The latter must not rush on to the offensive, as he must be prepared to undertake defensive responsibilities if the fast break fails.

The 1st trailer should take an active part in the offensive break and can fit into this role in many ways. As the three-lane break approaches the free-throw area, it may become temporarily halted by good defence on the part of the opposition. In this case the second wave of attack, by way of the 1st trailer, is brought into action. He may burst through the middle after calling 'ball right' or 'ball left', looking for a pass from whoever has the ball (Diagram 14), or if a shot has been taken, he is there to assist in rebounding. A variation of this is for the midde man on the break, as he is stopped by the defence, to pass to one of the cutters and then move in the same direction behind him looking for a return pass if the cutter is checked, whilst the 1st trailer replaces him on the free-throw line to maintain offensive balance.

In general, the two cutters should remain on their own sides of the court throughout and not cross under the basket in order to create balance and rebounding positions. On the other hand, three defensive players may have got back, but the break can still be pushed home if one cutter sets a screen by stopping on the side of the free-throw lane, and the other crosses under the basket and comes around from behind looking for a pass from the middle man. By crossing the court in this situation, he opens the way for the 1st trailer to fill the outside lane just vacated for a possible pass from the middle man, if the defence has followed the first cutter.

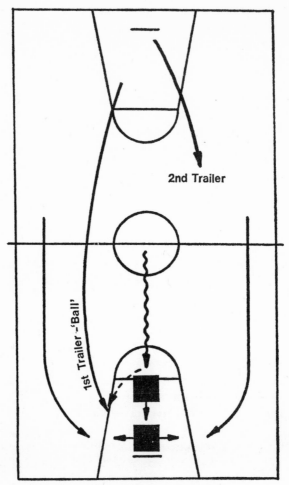

14. Second wave of attack

PRACTICES FOR THE FAST BREAK

1. A two-ball continuous practice involving a full-length dribble of the floor, finishing with a jump shot from outside the free-throw area (Diagram 15). Form two queues in diagonally opposite corners, and after the initial shots the shooters position themselves at each free-throw line in readiness to fight for the rebound from the next two shooters.

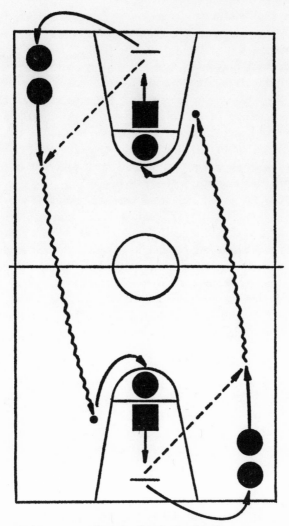

15. Practice for the fast break

Two players are contesting the rebound at each basket and the player who obtains the rebound makes an outlet pass to the next in line and joins the queue. The player who does not get the rebound, lines up on the inside position for the next rebound. Eight players are the minimum required to operate.

2. A two-ball continuous practice similar to that shown in the bottom half of Diagram 3, but using the full court and involving a lead pass and backing up by the trailing team-mate. Form two queues in diagonally opposite corners and have the first player in line break down court, signal, call for the ball and drive to the basket for a lay-up shot. The second player dribbles after the breaking player and, on hearing the signal, throws a lead pass and sprints down court either to tip the ball if the shot is missed or to rebound before the ball touches the floor. He then makes an outlet pass to the second player in line. Eight players are the minimum required to operate.

3. A continuous 3-on-2 fast-break practice going one way with a 2-on-1 (Diagram 16) break coming back. Form three queues behind the end line, one in the middle and one at each corner, with two players at the other end of the court in readiness to play defence. The players in the outer lanes remain at one end to form the next defence, whilst the former defenders break back up court after they have obtained the ball, with the middle player on the three-man break becoming the single defender. Eight players are the minimum required to operate continuously.

4. Rebounding and 3-on-2 fast-break practice. Three offensive and three defensive players position themselves at one basket. The coach or another player takes an outside shot, whilst the defence block out and rebound. Whichever team gains possession, they fast break against two defenders stationed at the other end. The two outer players on the break remain down court to act as defence for the next three attackers. Eleven players are the minimum required to operate successfully without time wasting.

5. Continuous 3-on-2 fast-break practice (Diagram 17). As the first three players move out on attack (players 4, 5 and 6), they are replaced by two players (10 and 11) to act as defence for the next wave coming back. Players 7 and 8 at the other end of the court play defence, and on gaining possession make an outlet pass to the first player in line (player 9) to start the next three-man break. Nine players are the minimum required to operate.

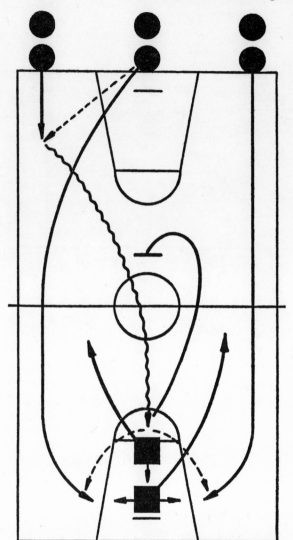

16. A continuous 3-on-2 fast break combined with a 2-on-1

Check points
* Possession and fast outlet pass.
* Communication and organisation of break.
* Ball to the middle.

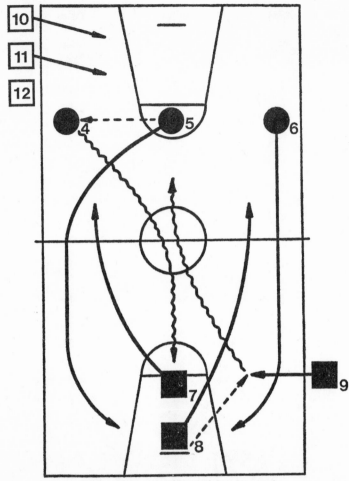

17. A continuous 3-on-2 fast break practice

* Recognition and application of correct options.
* Use of trailers.

THE ZONE OFFENCE

One of the basic principles of zone defence is for the defensive players to devote more attention to the ball than to the man. Emphasis, therefore, by the attacking team, should be initially on the fast break. The first wave of the break may not always bring the desired result, but it may serve to help organise the formation of the zone offence.

In preparing a zone offence, the coach should adapt his abilities to the needs of his players by providing an offence to suit the material at hand.

For a team to perform consistently throughout the season, it should be prepared soundly to meet all forms of defensive situations. In terms of a zone offence, the coach can make his decision in any one of three ways:

1. A separate offence to meet each zone formation,
2. An offence to take care of all zone variations, or
3. An all-purpose offence to meet all zones and, with slight modifications, be adaptable to meet man-for-man defences.

A separate offence for each zone formation would be asking too much of a team, especially with the limited time teams have for practice in this country, but problems may be reduced if the team is working for the 1-on-1 situation. The amount of time spent in preparing for separate offences would be tremendous, although the coach may compensate for this by changing the initial Guard position, but maintaining the basic manoeuvres of the offence. That is to say, if there are two men out front in defence (e.g. 2-1-2 zone), use one Guard in the basic offence. If there is one on defence (e.g. 1-3-1 zone), use two Guards in attack, thus creating 2-on-1 situations in which to exploit the defence. For effective results, the attacking team would have to be well drilled in the recognition of defensive formations and must have a good playmaker (Guard) in charge of floor activities, who should know which offensive formation to use against the defence presented.

Under the second method, adjustments would have to be made from the initial alignment, depending on the defensive formation. In other words, the offence will be dictated to by the defence, but still maintain individual freedom with control.

The third choice is a sounder proposition, as the coach has the great advantage of only having to teach one basic offensive formation which, with few modifications, is adaptable to meet a variety of defences, from zone to man-to-man and back again.

The Overload Offence

The emphasis in this form of offence is to get the ball and more offensive players into a part of the court than there are defensive players, in order to create 2-on-1 situations from which good shooting opportunities may arise. The attacking team, regardless of the type of defence encountered, must be patient and let the defence commit itself. When the zone shifts to cover overloading, players should cut into the open areas (Diagram 18). How well

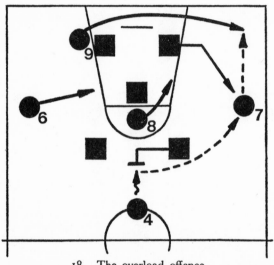

18. The overload offence

the attacking team can adjust to the defence being used is the secret of good offensive basketball. Overloading, when executed effectively, will present the offensive team with many middle-distance shooting opportunities, and it is essential for players to be capable of scoring these shots, in order to draw out the defence and open up the inside area.

The Wall Pass Against the Zone

One of the greatest dangers to any defence is a player cutting towards the basket looking for a pass. The 'wall pass' highlights this situation, as the zone defence places more accent on watching the ball than watching the offensive players. Zone defences are very vunerable to the simple 'pass the ball and go to the basket' manoeuvre as shown in Diagram 19, especially if the

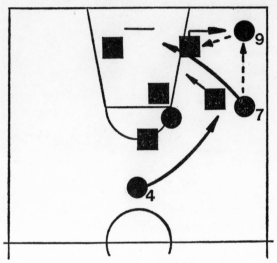

19. The wall pass against the zone

vacated area is filled by a team-mate. This kind of action, which can be used in every pass situation, does not afford the zone an opportunity to overplay the passing lanes and will create good shooting opportunities if the ball is passed rapidly.

MATCH UP OPPOSITE THE DEFENCE

As outlined earlier, if the defence is a 2-1-2 zone, use a single Guard in offence: a 1-3-1 formation, for example. If the zone is a 1-3-1 or 1-2-2, use two Guards in offence: either a 2-1-2 or 2-3 formation. This offence also makes use of the overload principle by stationing players in the gaps or open areas of the zone (Diagram 20) through which they can penetrate. This system forces the defence to adjust continually, and by passing

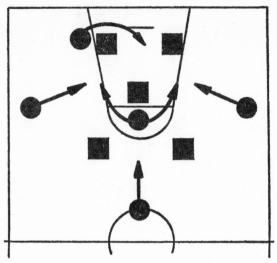

20. Match up opposite the defence

the ball to create further overloads it presents good shooting opportunities, as it is impossible for the defence to adjust as fast as the offence can.

Match Up With the Defence

If the defence is a 2-1-2 zone, use a 2-1-2 offence. If it is a 1-3-1 zone, use a 1-3-1 offensive alignment, etc. This puts the defence on a semi man-to-man basis, and establishes 1-on-1 situations which can exploit the weak spots in the defence by using manoeuvrability or size in personnel. As the ball is moved rapidly around the zone, the defence will be continually shifting, forming a kind of sagging man-for-man, until finally an individual opportunity presents itself or a shooting opportunity is created by the defensive sag.

Screen Plays Against the Zone

Screening is possible against zone defences and should be used whenever the opportunity presents itself, especially in the 2-on-1 situations which develop in the overload offence.

In order to build a sound zone offence a number of the points already discussed may be joined together to give the offence the necessary balance, and often for the personnel at hand the opportunity of expressing themselves individually.

The following points, not necessarily complete or in order of importance, are considered to be essential in producing a good zone offence.

1. Know why the opposition is using a zone defence. Most teams use a zone defence for specific reasons and these are highlighted in the chapter concerning Defence.

2. Do not allow the players to stand around too much in fixed positions, as the passing lanes can be cut off and the defence becomes more solid.

3. Work for good ball and player movement, along with good vision faking, which will shift the zone out of position. Often the best pass is a return pass.

4. Work for good rebounding balance. Many zones have their best rebounders under the basket, and the offence should counteract this by getting its best men in position to offset this advantage.

5. Be able to set up the good shooters on the overload principle, so that certain spot shooting instructions may be given (this also helps in practice).

6. Make the basic offensive manoeuvres simple enough to practice repetitively – repetition still being a good teacher.

7. Screening is possible against a zone and should be used, especially as the ball shifts from side to side (strongside/weakside).

8. Defensive balance must be maintained, especially if teams using the zone like to fast break.

9. Work on the baseline defenders. If a defender vacates his position, send a man into that area.

10. Make use of a high Post player. This allows greater flexibility of the zone offence and places pressure on most zone defences.

The following offence is described in detail to give a deeper understanding of the principles involved, and has been used extensively by the England (Under 19) Team with much success.

The offence is based on a 1-3-1 overload/rotation pattern and is used against any form of zone offence.

One of the first concerns in preparing a zone offence is the player placement and player movement. Player movement is necessary to place players in the position where they may do things they do best. In this 1-3-1 offensive formation, the key man is the Guard, O4 (Diagram 21). He selects where the

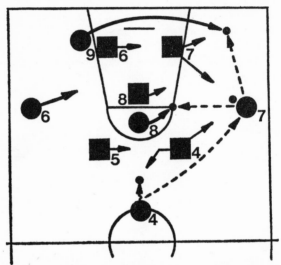

21. 1–3–1 overload/rotation pattern: initial options

offensive emphasis shall initially be directed, and with experience exploit the defensive weaknesses. 'He must be able to dribble well, move the ball, have a good outside shot to keep the defence honest and be capable of driving in the 1-on-1 situation.

At all times at least one player must be in this rear-court guard area to act as defensive balance on change of possession. The two Forwards, O6 and O7, must be spread to keep the middle open. They should be able to score from the outside to draw the defence, and be able to accept rear-court guard responsibilities when in this area. They should be good drivers and rebounders.

The high and low Post players, O8 and O9, should be tall,

Above: Palma (Mexico) starting his
~~ve~~ against Santillana (Spain).
~~te~~ Ramos (5) of Spain giving
~~port~~
Right: Two-handed rebound by
~~mo~~ (13) of Finland with a Canadian
~~at~~ his back in the 'outside' position

8. 'Wall pass' with No. 11 having passed the ball and cutting to the basket for a possible return pass from No. 6. Kings Norton v. Totton College

strong and tremendous offensive rebounders. They should possess a very good inside shot and be good ball-handlers.

Player placement should initially be as shown in Diagram 21, which also shows player movement and shooting opportunities when establishing the overload.

If O4 can penetrate to the top of the free-throw area, he should be prepared to shoot, with O8 and O9 taking up rebounding positions. If, as is usually the case, O4 is challenged much farther out by one of the Guards on defence, he should pass down the same side – to O7, in this case – through the defensive gap created. During this initial penetration, he should at all times be on the lookout for a possible pass to O9 under the basket for an easy two points.

Forwards O6 and O7 should manoeuvre themselves to receive the ball near the side line, free-throw line extended.

Low Post player O9 moves out to the corner to create the overload and establish the strongside, and in so doing looks to receive a pass under the basket on his way over if D7 is drawn to O7 on the initial Guard-to-Forward pass. High Post player O8 follows the ball to the corner of the free-throw area to complete the overload.

The first phase of the offence is based on the overload principle, with the establishment of good passing lanes and player penetration on 2-on-1 situations, looking for medium-range outside shots. Player O8 and O9, together with the non-shooting side Forward, should rebound all shots. It is important that each player establishes good floor balance (at least 4 to 5 metres between players) to create operating room for the player with the ball and to prevent a defensive player from defending two offensive players.

In order to maintain pressure on the defence, there should be player movement towards the basket (Diagram 22), and during this phase the emphasis is on the Forward cutting to the basket. As O7 passes the ball to O9 on the baseline, he cuts to the basket looking for a return pass, or O9 himself can look for the shot or go 1-on-1 down the baseline. To maintain offensive balance, O4 rotates to replace O7, and O6 replaces O4. If O7 does not receive a return pass, he continues through to the weakside and

D

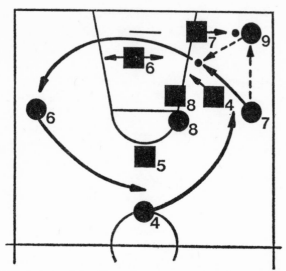

22. 1–3–1 overload/rotation pattern: secondary options

replaces O6. This move opens up the pass and cut possibilities, together with medium-range shooting, and to create even further pressure inside O8 should cut to the basket following in after O7, also looking for a pass from O9 or rebounding, as the case may be. If neither O7 nor O8 receives the ball, O8 should continue through to a low Post position on the weakside (Diagram 23).

As O7 cuts to the basket, he takes D4 with him part of the way, trying to prevent the return pass, thus opening up a gap into which O4 moves to take a pass from O9 for a possible medium-range shot, or he may go 1-on-1 as D4 tries to readjust. As O9 passes to O7, O8 or O4, he should always move towards the basket for rebound balance, which may also open up a further option of a return pass from O4 for a baseline shot.

If O4 is unable to gain a good shooting position, the ball is passed on to o6 moving into the rear-court guard area from the weakside, who may be in a good position to penetrate for a shot, due to the vacating of the high Post position by O8.

If no shooting opportunity presents itself, O6 passes the ball on to O7 as he emerges from behind the zone following his

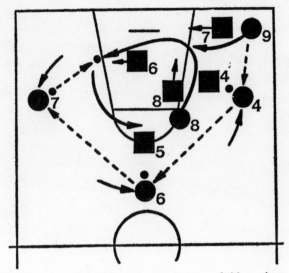

23. 1–3–1 overload/rotation pattern: weakside options

initial cut to the basket from the strongside. Provided that the ball is passed quickly from O9 and around the zone, this situation presents a very good shooting opportunity, as the zone is unable to adjust quickly enough. If D6 steps out to prevent the shot by O7, the ball is passed inside to O8 for a turn-around shot, or O8 may continue out and set a screen on D6 around which O7 can drive to free himself for a shot.

If none of these opportunities presents itself in a positive manner, continuity is maintained through the rotation, and offensive balance is ensured, thus preparing the offence for the pattern to be repeated. This offensive pattern (overload/rotation) can be worked down either side of the court, and depends mainly on which side the defence dictates the offence shall be worked initially (Guard-to-Forward pass). The ball should be made to do the work and shots should not be forced.

PRACTICES FOR ZONE OFFENCES

1. The teacher or coach, having formulated the team's zone offence, should first introduce the basic manoeuvres without defence.

When the team becomes proficient in what is expected from the offence, defence may be introduced. At this stage, perhaps only two or, at the most, three defenders are used in order to highlight some aspect of the offence. In this way, particular parts of the offence (two-and three-man plays) may be practised without the complications of full defensive pressure being exerted.

As the team becomes more proficient at offence, more defenders may be introduced until a 5-on-5 situation exists. Even at this stage, emphasis can be placed on the development of two- and three-man plays with continuity taking over should the offence break down.

2. A 5-on-5 half-court game with the attacking team having five or six separate attempts to score before changing over. Make the practice competitive by keeping score.

Check Points

* Maintaining offensive balance in terms of :
   (a) rebounding,
   (b) defence – safety man.
* Application of two- and three-man plays.
* Recognition of the correct options.
* Ability to score – first objective.

MAN-TO-MAN OFFENCE

Man-to-man offence is not played by choice, but is played because opponents have a free choice in deciding which defensive organisation they will use. It is therefore necessary for man-to-man offence to be an integral part of a team's playing repertoire. In addition to this, it is easier to build a man-to-man offence than it is to build a zone offence. The main reason is, of course, that man-to-man offence embodies the use of individual and pre-tactical skills which the players have used in their training and development. To knit these together requires less organisation than does zone offence. Man-to-man offence does not require the coach to prepare different types of offensive patterns, for the pattern adopted is sufficient to cater for strict or sagging man-to-man defences. Options within the pattern may vary slightly, but this will not alter the general organisation of the pattern.

The starting formation adopted is decided by the offensive team and can be retained because the defensive team will match the offensive positions wherever the offensive team station themselves; but in zone offence the defensive team dictate, to a certain extent, where the gaps to be attacked are. There is no possibility of an overload in the numerical sense because of the matching bias. The two principles of fitting the offence to the needs and abilities of the players, together with a balanced formation, bear repeating, and so it remains for the coach to organise a formation which will allow his team to make maximum use of the talents available.

CUTTING PLAYS

Cutting plays can be used to very good effect when the team is opposed by a man-to-man defence which is slow to move its feet or plays very tightly. The objective would be to incorporate movement of the ball and movement of players to create continuous 'wall pass' options. The movement of the players also caters for the necessary requirements of defensive balance and of keeping the middle free, which are requirements of all man-to-man offensive plays. A suitable formation and the movement required has already been outlined in Practice 1 at the end of the section on 'Relationship of Positions' in Chapter 4.

POST PLAYS

Post plays are not only the reserve of Post players. This pre-tactical skill can be used to very good effect between all players to cause a miss-match of abilities for the utilisation of 1-on-1 plays when switching occurs, or to produce an attacking player free with the ball when switching does not occur.

1-ON-1

Man-to-man defence, by its very nature, allows the use of many 1-on-1 opportunities, and maximum use of these situations should be encouraged as they present a threat to the whole defensive organisation. Good 1-on-1 play with the ball reduces the pressure on other attacking players because defenders who are working collectively will be seeking to help their colleagues. This produces opportunities for passing to attackers who are free, should not the 1-on-1 be successful in its own right.

Screen Plays

Screen plays are used to limited effect in adult basketball, since other methods of getting a player free are simpler and generally more effective. However, they can be particularly useful away from the ball and more so when close to the basket.

In the section Zone Offence there is a list of factors concerning the production of an offensive play. Many of those factors are relevant to man-to-man offence also, notably on knowing why the defence plays man-to-man, standing around, rebounding, simplicity, and defensive balance. One of the difficulties in man-to-man offence is the problem of allowing players complete freedom to move around. Usually this means that most players off the ball tend to fill the gaps near to the basket, creating a problem for any player getting free with the ball in restricting his possible drive to the basket. To alleviate this problem, it is suggested that coaches consider instructing offensive players not to trespass into anyone else's area unless they are involved with a two-man play, or are circulating to give defensive balance.

The following is an example of a man-to-man offence designed for a team which consists of average Post players, some good driving players and only one good outside shooter.

The starting line-up is shown in Diagram 24 together with the initial penetration attempts. Guard O5, the outside shooter, starts the movement with a pass to O7 and then cuts off the Post O8. This play creates a 1-on-1 opportunity for O7 or a return pass to the Guard (O5) or to the Post (O8) rolling to the basket. Failing that, a safety pass to O4, who has filled the gap, is made. O4 now has the opportunity of using the penetration and driving skills, since the middle is now free. A further pass to

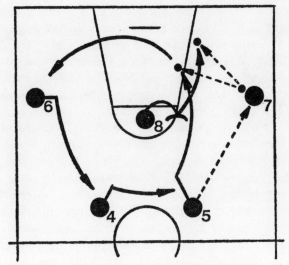

24. Man-to-man offence: initial options

O6 would enable a post play action to take place on the left-hand side if the Post has circulated into position. One additional pass would give the outside shooter, now on the weakside, a good outside shot. This is shown in Diagram 25 together with

25. Man-to-man offence: weakside options

the alternative of a screen play between O5 and O8 should the Post player be slow in circulating to the high Post position.

If these initial options do not produce satisfactory shooting opportunities, a further series of similar options can take place because the offensive movement has put the team back in the same formation. This simple play can be started down either side of the court with the circulation going the other way. Offensive rebounding is done by the Post player and whoever shoots. The rear-court Guard position is more than adequately covered to prevent fast breaks should the defence gain possession. The success of this offence demands good passing ability, particularly by the Forwards who are looking to feed the ball to cutting players in the middle. If the defence is strict, most of the shots will come from the side of the intitial penetration, but if the defence sags, the success is usually from the weakside.

With a slight modification to the basic organisation, the pattern can be used against zone defence, still allowing the strengths of the individual players to be used. The changes required would be for the outside players to revolve to create one Guard (O4), two Forwards (O5 and O6) and a baseline Forward (O7). The Post player would have similar duties as before in keeping the middle free and acting as a second move in any possible cutting plays.

Practice of man-to-man offence can be split into the various constituent parts and then the whole thing can be moulded together again.

When the first attempt at building an offence is made with beginners, the following advice will be of value.

Check Points

* Select the players for the various positions to allow use of specific skills and talents.

* Players must stay in their own area of operation unless they are involved in a two-man play or are circulating for defensive balance.

* The ball must not be held.

* When using wall passes and post plays, players must circulate to the opposite corner.

* Post players should not block the middle.

* The play is a means of getting one player free for an easy shot at the basket. In other words, a means to an end – not an end in itself.

Offence Against the Full-Court Press

Teams today are applying more and more full-court defensive pressure, and against the poorly prepared teams or those weak in the individual skills of the game, they are having tremendous success. If the opposition are operating a full-court press, it will generally only be applied after the opposition has scored, in order to give themselves time to organise.

This period of time also allows the team in possession to organise its offence against the press, and should be minimised by quickly establishing good floor positions, getting the ball in play fast and moving it up court rapidly before the opposition can fully organise its press.

The organisation of an offence against the full-court press can be achieved in many ways. If a team has a good, quick, ball-handling Guard, it may only be necessary to get the ball to this player who, through his own ability, can advance the ball up court on his own. But if he gets into difficulties, his teammates should be prepared to give him help immediately by freeing themselves to receive the ball. Remember the press favours the defence, as the team in possession have not only to maintain safe possession, but to advance the ball over the halfway line within 10 seconds and also attempt a shot within 30 seconds of gaining possession.

If teams don't have players with the necessary quickness and dribbling ability, they should not force this aspect of the game which only leads to turnovers, but organise themselves to advance the ball by creating good passing situations and not get caught in possession, which may lead to double-teaming.

The offence can be further organised by giving each player on court a specific responsibility and area in which to work. For example, the British Olympic Team organised its offence by detailing one of the big men to be solely responsible for putting the ball in play after a basket was scored. This player, having the necessary height to get the ball in play safely if pressured on the end line, and being able to move anywhere along the line to put the ball in play, should not get caught behind the backboard, as this might obstruct the in-bounds pass. Two other players were detailed to take up positions on each side of the court between the free-throw lane and sidelines, whilst the two Guards took up similar positions near the half-way line. As the ball was made ready to be passed in-bounds, the two players nearer the baseline went and screened for the Guards on their side of the floor and continued up court.

The ball was then passed to whichever Guard became free first, with the other Guard filling the middle lane and the in-bounds passer going down the opposite sideline to fill the outer lane. In this way the ball was advanced up court with the minimum of dribble and all players were a continual threat to the defence, as they were applying fast-break principles to a pressure situation, which caused the defence to make continual adjustments.

The offensive organisation also has to take into account the type of full-court press being used, be it zone or man-to-man. The zone press favours double-team traps and it is essential that the ball-handler does not get caught in a trap (see the section on pressing defences on pages 127–142). Against the zone press, screen situations to free players for the ball will not have the same success as against the man-to-man press, since the zone press is designed to defend against players in particular areas on court and not on an individual basis.

Once the ball has crossed the half-way line, the full-court press has effectively been broken, and unless teams can go to the basket without forcing the situation, they should control their play and quickly organise their half-court offence.

PRACTICES FOR OFFENCE AGAINST THE FULL-COURT PRESS

1. Firstly, introduce the basic movements without defence, then add a defensive player progressively as the attackers become more proficient, until the full 5-on-5 situation is reached.

2. It can be practised in conjunction with the team offence. One team practises the offence in a half-court situation, and

when they score they immediately apply the full-court press. The team initially on defence puts the ball in play from behind the end line and practises the press offence. Having reached the other end of the court, the whole process starts again with the same teams on offence and defence. Make it competitive by seeing which team scores the most in five or six attempts – one team in a half-court situation and the other going full-court against the press.

Check Points
* Individual confidence in each other's ability.
* Organise and get the ball in play quickly.
* Don't get caught in possession.
* Don't panic.

SPECIAL SITUATIONS

There are only a few situations within the game in which, because of their predictability specially organised plays can be put into practice to give some measure of success. In order for these to be effective, time is required for the deployment of players and the opposition have to be reasonably predictable in their movements. It may also be necessary for some form of signal to be given, so that all players are clear as to what action is required. These special situation plays are more common at international level than in our domestic basketball; but in close games at any level, a finely executed play in a given situation could ultimately effect the result in a team's favour.

Predictable situations occur within the game as follows:
(a) Jump ball at the beginning of the game and start of the second-half and extra periods.
(b) Jump ball at each free-throw restraining circle.
(c) Free-throws – offensive and defensive ends of the court.
(d) Out-of-bounds ball in the front-court.
(e) Out-of-bounds ball at the half-way line against a pressing defence.

JUMP BALL
Organisation for the jump ball situation can be divided into three parts: offensively if the tip looks like being won, defen-

sively if the tip looks like being lost, and the 50/50 possibility of it going either way.

Offensively

A jump ball at any of the three restraining circles can produce predictable circumstances from which a planned play can be performed if it can be seen that a team will get the tip. Generally, all players line up around the circle and, providing the jumping player can direct his tip to a team-mate, a predetermined play may be executed, resulting in a good possibility of scoring.

Defensively

Whenever players line up around the restraining circle for a jump ball, they should always position themselves on the defensive side of the opposition in order not to be caught at a disadvantage, should their team not gain possession from the tip. The four non-jumping players should note which way the opposing jumper is facing, as usually the ball will be tipped into the 180 degree area in front of the jumping player and adjustments can be made accordingly as the ball is tipped to defend against the opposition's gaining possession. The jumping player, unless he has a clear advantage, would have great difficulty in tipping the ball backwards, and therefore, to some extent, any player in this back position can be left undefended and greater pressure exerted on the remaining players. As the ball is tipped, care must be taken to go with any opponent who breaks out towards one's own basket, for if the opposition gained possession, it would be a relatively easy basket if the ball were then passed on to an undefended player breaking for the basket. In this respect teams are able to dictate the floor positions at a jump ball, but only when they position a player deep in their front court, as this must be guarded against and therefore draws a defensive player to offset the situation.

Two of the most important positions at a jump ball are those opposite each other on the restraining circle in line with the two baskets (Diagram 26). If a player is able to take up this position in his front court, great pressure is placed on the defensive team, usually resulting in the defence positioning a player on each side of him and thus relieving, to some extent,

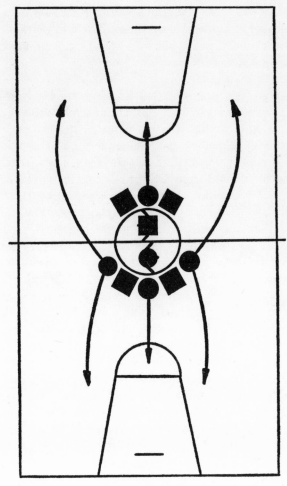

26. Jump ball

the pressure being applied to the other three non-jumping players. For the same reasons, it can be seen how important it is to take up a similar position in the rear court, thus denying the opposition the opportunity of exerting the same amount of pressure in reverse. By taking up these two key positions at the restraining circle, the opposition can be predicted in their movement fairly well, and should they obtain possession from the tip, three players are able to move immediately in defence. On the other hand, should possession go to the other team, three players again are able to move direct on offence.

FREE-THROWS

Player placement and player reaction at the free-throw situation depend whether the team is on offence or defence and whether the basket is scored or not. When a team is shooting free-throws, it is usual for at least two players to line up and contest the possible rebound from a missed second shot. The other two players usually position themselves laterally across court to prevent the possible outlet pass should the opposition gain posession; or they station themselves in tandem to delay the rush down court by harassing the ball-handler and at the same time retreating to the under-basket area until help arrives. Should the second shot be scored, the opposition still gain possession of the ball, but from behind the end-line which may be an ideal opportunity to consider using a full-court press. The relative position of each individual player is known and there is time in which to organise the defence.

The team defending against free-throws should always line up their two best rebounders on the inside position, who should be capable of blocking out the opposition before rebounding the missed second shot. If possession is obtained in this situation, a well-organised team can immediately gain the advantage and go to their fast-break play discussed earlier in this chapter. This is also true if the second shot is scored, provided that one of the would-be rebounders is designated to step quickly out of court with the ball and put it into play immediately, thus striking quickly before the defence has time to organise.

On the second free-throw, a third player should line up on the free-throw line and be responsible for rebounding in the middle area and denying the ball back to the shooter should the shot be missed. The remaining two players may station themselves at predetermined positions – which may be down the sides behind the rebounders or even in their opponents' half – so as to apply pressure immediately when possession is gained. In the former position the rebounders may gain a little advantage in knowing they have support behind them, and therefore, instead of having to catch the ball, may elect to tap it forwards or backwards to their team-mates in the corners.

OUT-OF-BOUNDS BALL

Out-of-bounds plays are used extensively in International basketball and are becoming more widely used in this country at club level. These plays are mainly used in a team's front court for two reasons :

(a) To provide an immediate shot at basket, and

(b) To provide a safe means of getting the ball in court when confronted with the pressure of a 5–on–4 situation.

Offensively, the team has time to organise itself and take up predetermined positions on the court, thus making the defence commit itself and therefore making it predictable. On a given signal, usually as the referee hands over the ball to the in-bounds passer, certain pre-planned manoeuvres take place to free a player to receive the ball and gain a good opportunity to shoot and score. Against both man-to-man and zone defences, this usually involves some form of screen play to free a player for the initial pass and shot.

When confronted by pressure in the late stages of a game and opting for possession instead of shots, it may be difficult to make the in-bounds pass due to the 5–on–4 player advantage of the defence. In this case, an out-of-bounds play at the half-way line would be extremely useful, although space is on the side of the in-bound passer's team, as the whole court may be used to their advantage; whereas the situations detailed earlier are restricted to the front court only, with the ball not being allowed back over the half-way line.

PRACTICES FOR SPECIAL SITUATIONS

1. Special situation plays can be introduced in the same way as the offence – initially without defence until the players are familiar with the movements involved. Each situation can be practised in isolation from the others and the defence should be

introduced very early in their development, as many situation plays depend on the reactions of the defence.

2. Whenever team plays are being practised either defensively or offensively, situation plays can be introduced as the occasions arise.

7. *Tactical Skills — Defence*

FAST-BREAK DEFENCE

If a fast break develops as a result of an interception or if a loose ball is picked up, very little can be done in the way of defence. These situations usually involve one attacker and all that can be done is to change as quickly as possible from offence to defence and attempt to overhaul the opponent. If a defensive player has managed to get back in time, he should force the opponent away from the basket and fight a delaying action until help arrives. He should not challenge the attacker in the mid-court area, as to fail in this situation opens the way to goal, but should immediately head for the under-basket area to prevent an uncontested lay-up shot.

Defence against the fast break should be aimed at the type which is controlled and organised, resulting from a basket made or rebound after an unsuccessful attempt. In these situations definite instructions may be given and practised.

The first line of defence against the fast break should be fought on the opposition's backboard. A team's offence should include rebound balance to help to minimise the effectiveness of the fast break by creating movement towards the basket – so as to establish good rebounding position. Prevent the defence from taking uncontested rebounds, as this helps them in setting up the fast break. Fight for position the instant a team-mate releases the ball on a scoring attempt, and rebound aggressively.

If the opposition obtains possession, the rebounder should be continually harassed by the nearest offensive player, or even double-teamed, so as to prevent the quick release of the outlet pass. If the outlet pass is prevented or substantially delayed, the fast break is unable to develop.

As the ball is rebounded by the opposition, an immediate transition from offence to defence should take place. Any delay at this stage may permit an opponent to gain the slight advantage necessary to push home the fast break.

A team's offence should have floor balance to include at least one player at all times, in the rear-court guard area for defensive balance, and to act as safety man against the fast break.

If a fast-breaking team has definite areas into which the outlet pass is constantly made, move to intercept or prevent these passes, thus disrupting the initial organisation of the break. No doubt teams have optional areas in which to make the outlet pass, but if access to the preferred area is prevented, the threat or the fast break is weakened. If, however, the outlet pass is received, continual harassment of the ball-handler should be maintained for the purpose of delaying the break.

Once the break gets under way and the defence are hustling back down court, continual pressure should be applied to the dribbling player to try to change his direction, or preferably to make him pick up the ball. The defence should be attempting to beat the ball down court and at the same time looking to intercept passes.

2–ON–1 DEFENCE

Should the offence get two or more lanes of attack down court with only one player back on defence, the defender should fight a delaying action and play for time by retreating to the free-throw lane area, never letting the offence get ahead of him and making the dribbler pick up the ball by faking to challenge, and then quickly stepping back to cover the cutter (see Diagram 12 on the Fast Break). The defender should offer the outside shot, but never the lay-up; and the more passes the offence can make before the shot, the more time there is available for help to get back on defence.

3–ON–2 DEFENCE (TANDEM)

If a 3-on-2 situation is created by the fast break, the two defensive players must quickly retreat to the free-throw lane area and not challenge in mid-court (see Diagram 13 on the Fast Break). The defensive players take up TANDEM positions (one behind the other), as playing side by side would make it too easy for the offence to split them on the drive. The tandem defence is essential if the under-basket shot is to be prevented, and it also offers good positioning for communication between the two. It is designed to prevent the uncontested lay-up shot and to delay the opposition from scoring whilst help is on its way.

The front man on defence attempts to make the ball-handler, as he approaches the top of the free-throw lane, pick up the ball or make a pass to one of the cutters. The defender can do this by faking a challenge at the ball or actually committing himself to pressurising the dribbler. As this is accomplished, he immediately falls back to the under-basket area just vacated by his team-mate, who has challenged the pass receiver. The top player, as he takes up his new position, should prevent or intercept any cross-court pass from one cutter to the other, and if the ball is passed back to the middle man on the break, he should quickly decide whether to challenge or block out the cutter on his side of the court whilst his team-mate does the same, thus preventing the under-basket shot.

At all times the tandem alignment should confront the ball and on no account should the cutters be allowed to shoot, as this generally is an easier shot than one from the free-throw line area. In cases where the ball is advanced down the side of the court and not the middle, the same tandem alignment should confront the ball-handler, and again the middle man on the break should be offered the outside shot, but not the cutters.

MAN-TO-MAN DEFENCE

The principles of team defence should be studied before any decision is made upon which type of team defence is to be adopted by the coach. These principles are :

1. To prevent penetration of the ball into the high percentage scoring areas.

2. To discourage shooting from the high percentage scoring areas.

3. To have support in depth.

4. To obtain defensive rebounds and capitalise upon the change of possession.

5. To match the talent of the opposition.

6. To match the patterns of the opposition's team play.

Man-to-man defence is a further extension of individual and pre-tactical defensive play. Each defensive player is assigned to defend an opponent and reacts according to the situation he is in, whether it be 'on' the ball or 'off' the ball.

At the same time he combines with team-mates to reduce the effectiveness of any two-man plays which are in progress. The individual defender's main responsibility, however, is his assigned opponent and he should be prepared to deny the opponent the individual options available and to block out and secure any rebounds the opponent tries to take. In addition to this there is a collective responsibility to help team-mates who are in trouble and also to provide the team with defence in depth. It will be obvious that with this form of defence, the offence dictates to a certain extent where the defensive players stand or move. This, however, can be minimised by good individual and collective defensive play. In a typical situation of the ball being advanced down the middle area of the court, the defensive positions are as shown in Diagram 27. The player responsible for the ball-handler would attempt to stop the dribble, or at least steer his man to the side or to the middle where help could be called upon either in the form of the sideline, or other defensive team-mates. The individuals defending attacking players, close to the ball, including the Post player, would be positioned to discourage the pass, and the players farther away would be sagging off their respective attacking players to provide support in depth, thus blocking the middle to discourage any possible drives and passes into that region.

There are guide lines which players in a man-to-man

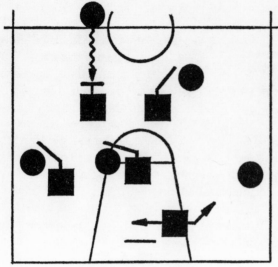

27. Man-to-man defence

defence can adopt to help them be more efficient as a collective unit when defending against covergent plays. The first of these guide lines is that there should be no 'sliding' within shooting distance when the convergent play concerns the ball. Away from the ball, however, it is not so critical. The second guide line is that 'switching', which may cause a mis-match, should not be permitted, particularly within shooting range. Having given these guide lines, it bears repeating that the collective responsibility of the team is not to allow attacking players their freedom with the ball. This means that defenders *should* 'switch' on convergent plays if an attacking player is going to be successful in freeing himself in a situation that would give him an unmolested shot. Finally, no attacking player should be given the opportunity of driving for the basket undefended, and so in the last resort the nearest defender should 'switch' assignments even though there is no one to 'switch' assignments with. There are instances in which 'sliding' and 'switching' do not cause hardship, as in the case of an attacking team which uses two Guards converging, or as part of its team play. Since one of the principles of team play is to match talent, every effort should be made by defensive players to stick to their assignments.

As the ball is moved around, so the defensive players positions would change accordingly. When attacking players move, the defending players would try to maintain a position which enables them to fulfil their collective responsibilities.

In man-to-man defence where there is movement by defensive players all around the defensive playing area, defenders can help each other into good defensive situations by verbal communication and by physical assistance, particularly in screen and post plays where 'switching' and 'sliding' will be in evidence.

Normally, responsibilities for attacking players do not change, and 'stick' should be the order of the day. If attacking players are using screens and post plays it may be necessary to 'switch' and 'slide', in which case there must be a rapid reassignment of responsibilities. Theoretically, then, each offensive player is defended all the time and therefore, in a rebound situation, all attacking players are blocked out and the defensive rebound should be secured.

There are a number of general instructions which will help teachers and coaches in developing a team to show good positional play in man-to-man defence:

1. Watch the man and see the ball.

2. The nearer the attacker is to the ball, the nearer will be the defender to block the passing and driving lanes.

3. The farther the attacker is from the ball, the more the defender will sag to block the passing and driving lanes.

4. Post players are defended closely all the time whilst they are in that position.

The strengths of a man-to-man defence are more numerous than those of a zone defence and it is suggested that man-to-man defence is the *primary* team defence, particularly with beginners. These strengths are:

1. Each individual in the defence has a clearly defined responsibility.

2. Since all defence depends on the success of the 1-on-1 and 2-on-2 situations, the 1-on-1 and 2-on-2 defensive situations can be practised on their own.

3. There are more defenders on the 'inside' position during rebounds.

4. The attacking player is defended all the time whilst within shooting range.

5. It is easier to match talent.

6. The offensive patterns are matched by the defence due to the individual assignments.

In the first stages of practising man-to-man team defence it is recommended that 'strict' man-to-man defence should be enforced, so that beginners have a chance to develop a pride in their achievements and to learn what their responsibilities are by a gradual process. It is sufficient to play within the shooting range of the opponents, for to play farther out than that would be too demanding and less effective.

However, when the responsibilities have been learned, the individuals within the team can extend their scope to include the collective responsibilities mentioned previously. This would be known as 'sagging' man-to-man defence. The third stage of development would be to extend the 'strict' man-to-man defence over a wider area of the court than the shooting range of the attackers. This stage means that the team is progressing towards the 'Press', which is dealt with later.

ZONE DEFENCE

The principles of defence remain the same whatever type of defence is used, but just as there are certain strengths (and weaknesses) in man-to-man defence, so there are in a zone defence and it is the tactical considerations which decide which type of defence shall be used.

Zone defence is the term used to describe the alternate means of defending the shooting area. Man-to-man defence indicates that the same defender plays against an attacking player all the time. In zone defence it is different. The zone is that area between the ball on the periphery of the shooting area and the basket. To cover this area effectively, the zone defence organises itself in a shape which will attempt to fulfil the principles of defence whilst occupying that area.

This is a fairly easy thing to do. Since the ball is the object that the zone is concerned with, the shape and movement of the zone should be relative to the movements of the ball. Other literature on this subject tends to position the zone in relation to the basket, and as the basket is static so are many zone defences. The more static they are, the easier they are to penetrate. In teaching beginners zone defence, it is important that they are introduced to it realising that their movement within the zone will be relative to the ball AND to opposing players. It must not be forgotten that it is players who score and not spaces. The first objective in the zone is to prevent the penetration of the ball. This is done by a defending player making himself responsible for the attacker with the ball. Behind this situation the other players organise themselves into a shape which will cover the shooting area and the attacking players within it most effectively. One of the most effective shapes is the 'Umbrella' shape (see Diagram 28). The most important

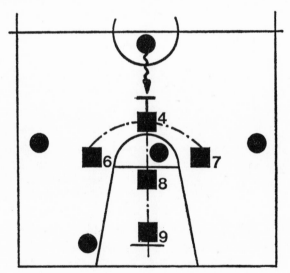

28.   Zone defence: 'umbrella' shape

aspect of this is that it is *relative to the ball*. The duties of the various players within the zone are as follows :

Player D4	to stop the penetration of the ball-handler.
Players D6 and D7	to support D4 on their side of the court and to be responsible for the first attacking player from the ball on their side.
Player D8	to support D4 from behind (support in depth) and to be responsible for any high Post player, discouraging any passes into that area.
Player D9	–to give greater support in depth, being responsible for any baseline attackers and to protect the basket.

If all defenders fulfil the obligations of their role and a pass to the side is made, the zone will move accordingly, maintaining its shape RELATIVE TO THE BALL, but responsibilities of individuals will change (*see Diagram* 29).

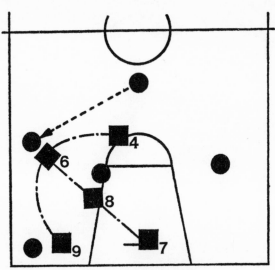

29. Zone defence: shape relative to the ball

The responsibilities are now :

Player D6	to stop the forward penetration of the ball.

Player D9	to support D6 on that side of the court.
Player D4	to support D6 and help to protect the high Post area.
Player D8	continues to discourage the ball being passed 'inside'.
Player D7	moves towards the under-basket area and accepts responsibility for protecting the basket and covering the weakside.

Diagram 30 shows what movement the defence would make

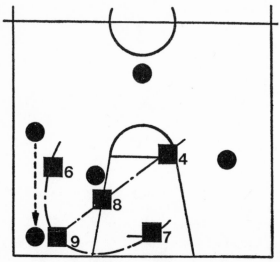

30.   Zone defence: pass into the corner

if a further pass was made into the corner. The responsibilities here are repeated, but again attached to different players.

The apparent weakness which shows in the diagram is that the player farthest from the ball in each case is not defended closely. However, because he is the farthest from the ball, a pass would take time and this would be time enough for the defence to readjust.

One additional item which is apparent is that the movement of players from the original 'line-up' is unrestricted in terms of area, and is dependent upon the movement of the ball. Through this, a more effective team defence is obtained, but because it does require more movement, co-ordination and communication within the zone are of paramount importance, particularly when attacking players without the ball run through the zone. When this happens, defensive players should still accept the individual responsibility by staying with the attacker until the attacker moves into the next defender's region, when responsibility will be transferred. Should the ball be passed to an attacking player within the zone area, then the attacking player can be challenged from both front and back by having the zone collapse from where the ball came from to the point where it is. This should then force the ball out again.

The use of a shape to define a zone defence has advantages. The first is that the players within the zone find it easier to recognise where they should be, in relation to each other, and this is particularly important when the defence tries to retain its shape relative to the ball, wherever the ball may be: visual impressions (i.e. the shape) are always a more effective aid to understanding than verbal expressions. The second advantage is that roles are clearly defined, this again bears in mind the beginner.

The strengths of this type of zone defence are as follows:

1. Penetration to close-in positions for shooting is difficult because there is considerable defence in depth as well as individual responsibility.

2. It forces the attacking team to shoot from outside.

3. Whenever a shot is taken there are always four players in the rebound area, in particular the tall players.

4. On a change of possession the fast break is very much easier to organise because of the defined positions of the defence.

5. The defence to some extent dictates where the offence shall stand or move.

6. The 'pride' of individual defence is retained, even though opponents and defensive duties will change rapidly.

7. A tall Post player can be double teamed.

The practice of zone defence cannot be broken down into small parts. It relies very heavily on good individual defence though, and this can be practised in 1-on-1 and 2-on-2 situa-

tions. However, the CHECK POINTS which need to be brought out when practising as a team are :
* Make sure there is a man on the ball.
* There is defence in depth.
* There is movement of the zone to retain its shape in relation to the ball.
* The Post player is defended.
* There is verbal communication between players resulting in a more co-ordinated team defence.

The defence described relates to one particular shape. Priorities may dictate that other shapes are used to form a zone defence. In the Umbrella zone defence it is seen that the front defender commits himself to the ball and the shape is taken up from that committal, whether the ball was advanced down the middle of the court or the side. It is possible that the ball does not need to be defended so closely by one defender and that two players forming a broad front may be sufficient, each one attacking the ball from his respective side, thus preventing penetration between them. Such a shape could be called the 'Box' shape defence, with the objective being to present a side of the box to the ball, as the ball is moved round the zone. The corners of the box would act as pincers on the ball. Again, the shape of the defence could be kept relative to the ball, and positions and movements are shown in Diagram 31 and 32. Other shapes which would be useful aids to developing zone defences are the 'Wedge' and the 'Blunt Wedge'.

This new concept of using shapes to teach, coach and develop zone defences instead of the numerical notation used in other literature has considerable advantages. Firstly, defenders do not have to be taught where to move in each of the many different situations which occur, they move naturally when trying to organise the readjustment of the shape. Secondly, it improves the collective co-operation of players with each other, which is essential in a good zone defence. It must be remembered that the movement they make is relative to the ball and the shape they are trying to keep. This does not leave players standing in a position on court doing nothing when the ball is on the opposite side of the court, as they usually do when

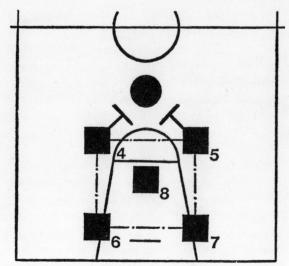

31. Zone defence: 'box shape' positions and movements

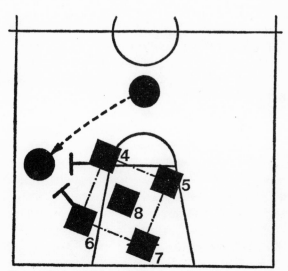

32. Zone defence: positions and movements relative to the ball

given a space to defend. A more mobile defence is a better defence.

One of the main disadvantages of the numerical notation is that it is only a notation for the starting positions. Once the ball is moved around a zone, the positioning of the players at any one stage usually bears little relation to the original numerical formula, and as such the strengths of the zone defence could be lost. With this new method, the strengths of a zone defence are kept intact.

The Use of Team Defences

Coaches and teachers alike will often be in a position of uncertainty regarding the use of the various types of defence. It is a decision the coach makes on his own, but there are principles upon which this decision can be made. With regard to beginners, if practice and class sessions are planned and carried out correctly, they should be getting a lot of practice at individual and pre-tactical defence. This in itself would suggest that man-to-man team defence is the easiest to organise, and also the best considering the talent available. As abilities improve, then tactical considerations have an effect on the choice.

Generally speaking, man-to-man defence encourages attacking players to drive, particularly those who are faced with a weak defender. Zone defences are more likely to give the opposition easier outside scoring shots. In either case, failure to contend with the problem ought to produce a change of personnel or a change in the type of defence used. It is a question of looking at the strengths and weaknesses of the opponents' talent and team play and the assessment of one's own talent and team defensive ability, and then making decisions which will reduce the opponents' degree of success.

The whole question revolves around the assessment of relative strengths and weaknesses. If a team has a very good fast break, then a zone defence would produce a more stable organisation to launch it from, but if the opponents are scoring from outside shots all the time, the zone defence is not much use. If a team has poor shooters from outside, but has an exceptionally good player, then they should not be encouraged to drive inside by playing strict man-to-man defence. It may only be necessary to play a sagging man-to-man defence so that the opponents' 'star' can be defended tightly all the time by offering support in depth.

PRESSURE DEFENCES

Not so long ago, the only time pressure defences were used was late in a game when a team was apparently beaten and resorted to the Press in an attempt to get back in the game. More recently, nationally prominent teams in the U.S.A. and Europe have demonstrated the possibilities of pressing tactics, so much so that teams are now effectively pressing for the whole game. As a result, the press in one form or another has become a prevalent part of a team's defensive play and at beginner level is most effective.

For the press to be effective, players must develop the qualities of speed, lateral quickness, good co-ordination, fitness, and an aggressive and determined spirit allied with extremely good individual defensive techniques.

The press should aim at demoralising and disorganising opponents by causing them to rush their offence, throw wild and careless passes, and to commit rule violations, all of which present the pressing team with more opportunities for possession and thus to score. The press upsets the timing and smoothness of an opponent's normal offence and, when effective, reduces the offensive potential of an opponent. A pressing defence is often used against a slow mechanical team, poor ball-handlers and those slow-breaking teams not prepared to meet such a defence. Through the use of a pressing defence, many more fast-break opportunities arise from interceptions, and a fast-breaking team should have pressure defence as part of its defensive repertoire.

Regardless of the type of press employed, the following objectives should be maintained and can be applied to a full, three-quarter or half-court situation.

1. To force a team away from its normal style of play by upsetting the timing and usual operating positions of the offensive players.

2. To take the game to the opposition in order that speed, quickness and agility become more important than sheer height.

3. To force a team into committing mistakes such as bad passes, double dribbles, etc., which offer more scoring opportunities for the pressing team.

4. To create confusion in the opposing team's offence, and in this way, the press becomes a potent means of attack.

MAN-TO-MAN PRESSES

When applying a full court man-to-man press, the opposition are picked up on an individual basis wherever they may be immediately on the change of possession (instant defensive obedience), and defensive pressure is applied to all players as long as the offence maintain possession of the ball.

Each player will know his defensive assignment and should, where possible, be matched to equalise height, speed and agility. In general, the taller, slower players should pick up the opposing players nearer their own basket, whilst the smaller, quicker players shoud harass the opposition in the front court and do the bulk of the chasing. One of the defending taller players, who may be the slowest man on the team, should be given basket protection responsibilities. Since pressing is, to some extent, a gamble, at least one player should be responsible for defending the basket against a possible breakdown in defence. This player may permit outside shots, but under no circumstances should he allow the opposition an uncontested lay-up shot.

In general, it is the responsibility of all players to stick with their assignments, but if the opposition are a quick-breaking team they may have difficulty in locating their assignments after a rebound, interception or other change in possession from the field of play. In this case it may be better to play a half-court defence, which offers time to get back on defence after first containing the initial push of the opposition, and only go full-court when the pressing team has time to organise.

9. Screen play set by Naylor (14) and accepted by Bayes (21), having screened off Rowland (5). Doncaster Panthers v. England U. 19 Squad

10. Gattorna (11) on a 1-on-1 drive against Kaaba (14) at the end of a fast break. Wilson Panthers v. Manchester

11. Good blocking out by the Portuguese team (white shorts) eliminates some of height and positional advantages of the England team

12. Peychev (14) of Bulgaria blocking out at a free-throw situation. Note the movement of the feet

Ideally these occasions arise from the following situations :
(a) Following a basket from the floor.
(b) Following a successful second free-throw.
(c) Following an offensive violation or foul in the front court.
(d) Following a time-out or substitution where the ball is brought into play in the front court.

At all times pressure should be maintained on the ball-handler, forcing him towards the sideline, as these lines favour the defence. Therefore, it is to the advantage of the defence to make use of the sidelines whenever possible. The press will not be effective unless each player is alert and prepared to apply pressure at all times, on and off the ball.

Defensive players should position themselves to the inside (off-line defence), which in effect forces the play to the outside. Position is important and, if near the ball, they should be close enough to discourage or intercept passes, but not so close as to be faked out of position or cause fouls to be committed.

They should make use of their peripheral vision and always position themselves to see both the ball and their opponent. Players far away from the ball need not be so tight on their men, but should be looking to give assistance where necessary and always sag toward the ball so as to block the passing and driving lanes. When an attacking player has had his dribble and picked up the ball, he should be harassed by the defensive player in order to make him throw a bad pass, whilst those defensive players nearest the ball should tighten up on their men to discourage the pass being made. In this way a 5-second call may be made resulting in jump ball, or he may be forced into throwing a long pass which could be intercepted (Diagram 33).

Players should endeavour to make the dribbler pick up the ball at all times and attempt to prevent his forward progression down court by good positional play. If a defensive man is beaten this should be communicated to the rest of the team and help given by those backing up, who would pick up the loose man quickly and aggressively. The beaten man, instead of chasing his assignment, would be looking to pick up the spare

E

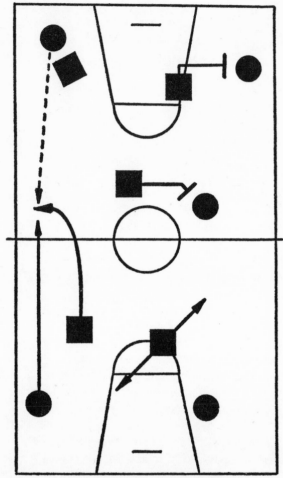

33. Man-to-man presses: interception

man and keeping watch on the ball at the same time in case a pass is made to the player just vacated (Diagram 34). If the attacking players in their back-court attempt screening in order to free themselves on the dribble, this opens up double-teaming possibilities and should be exploited. On the other hand, if they are screening to free a player for a pass, the defensive players, if unable to escape the screen, should switch assignments quickly

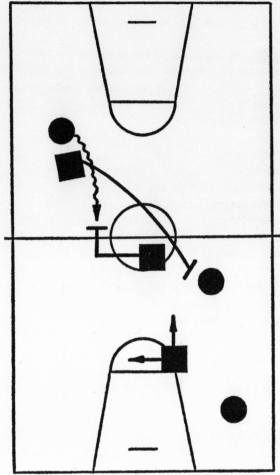

34. Man-to-man presses: switching

and aggressively to maintain pressure. When an opponent with the ball stops in a vulnerable position, he should be double-teamed, especially if he is on the sideline or in a corner of the court. In this situation, the remaining players would over-play the attackers nearest the ball to deny the easy pass.

As mentioned earlier, the full-court press is difficult to employ except after a basket or a delay for a violation, time-out or an out-of-bounds ball. If the ball is rebounded or intercepted, there is not sufficient time to get the full-court press organised. This is where the half-court press would be more effective by quickly dropping back into the rear court and then moving to pick up players as they cross the half-way line. A combination of the full- and half-court presses, applied under the same basic principles outlined, would make it possible for a team to press effectively on every play situation.

ZONE PRESSES

The zone press differs from that of the man-to-man press in that the defensive players are located in and are responsible for defending players in a particular area on court.

They defend all players within their area and are continually looking to double-team the opposition in specific situations.

Although the objectives of the zone press are the same as those for man-to-man, they are more specific and need to be established for the press to be effective. The following are the most functional objectives of the zone press :

1. Force the ball-handler into a bad pass situation.
2. Tie up the ball-handler to force a 5-second held ball situation.
3. Force the opposition into making rule violations.
4. Force the opposition into making high, long or cross-court passes, in order that interceptions or deflections can be made.
5. Steal the ball from the opposition whenever possible.

The zone press can be operated on a full, three-quarter and half-court basis, and to accomplish these objectives pressure must be exerted on the ball-handler at all times, while cutting off the passing lanes to his colleagues. Pressure on the ball is achieved by double-teaming the ball-handler at each successive position, and this is carried out by rushing two defensive players at the man with the ball, trying to put him in a panic situation. The defenders should be so positioned as to force the ball-handler into a trap between the two, preventing his forward movement down court and making him pass over the defence.

It is absolutely vital that the double-teamers prevent the

ball-handler from splitting them on the dribble, as this would put a heavy load on the remaining defensive players trying to cover the huge gaps thus created by this defensive mistake. By being deceptive in their approach, the double-teamers can establish good positions and should attempt to wedge the opponent with the ball into a 'V', which is close enough at the point to discourage the dribble. The defence should make the dribbler pick up the ball, but if he attempts to dribble out of the trap, the defensive players should adjust their positions by closing the gap.

Once the double-team has been set, they maintain their position as close as possible without making contact (no fouls) and by waving and keeping their arms high, trying to deflect the ball or cause a lob pass to be made which can be intercepted by a team-mate.

HALF-COURT ZONE PRESS

The principle of double-teaming the ball-handler can be applied to a number of pressure defences of differing formations. To illustrate this, the 1–2–2 half-court zone press is one defence employing these tactics.

For clarity and better understanding, the half court is divided into five areas and a defensive player assigned to each. Whichever area a defensive player finds himself in, he will take on the defensive responsibilities assigned to that area, be it CHASER (player 5,) CONTAINER (players 6 and 7) or PROTECTOR (players 8 and 9). This will provide for better communications when referring to defensive positions.

The object of this defensive alignment is to create four positions at which the double-team trap can be effected (Diagram 35), making use of the sidelines and corners where possible, but at all times denying the ball to the middle. The Chaser along with one Container will effectively trap out front, and a Container and Protector will trap down the sides and corners.

Once the player positions are understood, each player should be familiar with the responsibilities of the other players for complete understanding of the press.

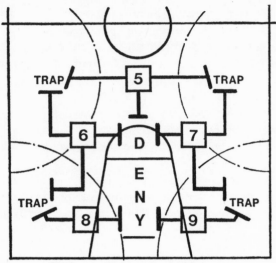

35. Half-court zone press: double team traps

PLAYER RESPONSIBILITIES (Diagrams 36 and 37)
Chaser (5)
1. Guide the direction of a pass or the dribbler to a position favourable to the defence.

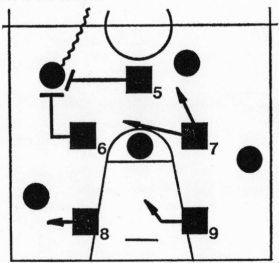

36. Half-court zone press: player responsibilities I

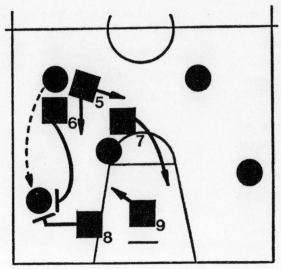

37. Half-court zone press: player responsibilities II

2. Double-team the man in possession when the ball is out front to the left or right.

3. Protect the middle area of the press when the ball is down the sides or in a deep position.

4. Anticipate and deflect or intercept any pass within range.

Containers (6 and 7)

1. Guide the direction of the ball-handler into the front trap.

2. Contain the dribbler by preventing his progression down the sides of the court.

3. Double-team the man with the ball when he is:

(a) on his side of the court out front, or

(b) on his side of the court at the side or corner position.

4. Deny the free-throw line area when the ball is out front on the opposite side of the court.

5. Protect the under-basket area when the ball is down the opposite side or in the corner, and rebound aggressively.

Protectors (8 and 9)

1. Protect the under-basket area against long or short passes.

2. Double-team the man with the ball down his side of the court.

3. Protect against the Post and free-throw lane area when the ball is down the opposite side or in the corner, and rebound aggressively.

All Players

1. Don't allow the dribbler to penetrate the zone.
2. Don't allow the ball to reach the free-throw line area. If this happens, collapse on the ball immediately and force it out of this vulnerable position.
3. Don't expose the under-basket area.
4. FAST BREAK on all possessions gained.

FULL-COURT ZONE PRESS

The full-court zone press operates under the same basic principles and can be said to be an extension of the half-court defence, although full-court pressure requires more time to organise, since the players are deployed all over the court. For this reason, it is best used when there is a delay in the change from offence to defence (see Man-to-Man Presses page 129).

The full-court zone press can have many basic alignments, each producing double-team situations to keep constant pressure on the ball, which reduces the effectiveness of a screening offence and will cause many bad passes and violations to occur.

A typical full-court zone press is the 1–2–1–1 formation which provides good floor balance and offers control of the passing lanes. Again the court is divided into five areas with a defensive player assigned to each. By naming the areas again, defensive responsibilities are better explained, and it helps to overcome communication difficulties between players on court.

The press involves one CHASER (player 5) two CONTAINERS (players 6 and 7) an INTERCEPTOR (player 8) and a PROTECTOR (player 9), who aim to create four positions in the front court at which the double-team trap can be effected (Diagram 38). As the ball is brought into play, the Chaser and one of the Containers look to double-team in the 1st Trap Area, whilst the remaining players overplay the passing lanes. Where possible, the ball should be brought into play down the left-hand side of the court, away from the trailing Official so as to minimise the number of fouls called. If the

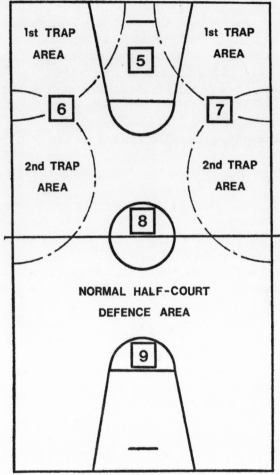

1st TRAP AREA

5

1st TRAP AREA

6

7

2nd TRAP AREA

2nd TRAP AREA

8

NORMAL HALF-COURT DEFENCE AREA

9

38. Full-court zone press

ball is advanced past the front line of defence, a second double-team should be effected in the 2nd Trap Area by the Interceptor and Container nearest the ball, whilst the remaining players fall back covering the passing lanes. Once the ball has crossed the half-way line, the defensive players should regroup and take up their normal half-court defence, as continuing to trap effectively may be difficult once the offence is on the move. This defence is designed to produce opportunities of gaining possession in the front court, which is a choice scoring area. As the ball penetrates to the back court, the defence may pick up in a man-to-man defence or coverage on the basket and play some form of zone defence. The Umbrella zone formation, for example, lends itself quite readily to this application.

PLAYER RESPONSIBILITIES (Diagrams 39, 40 and 41)
Chaser (5)
1. Guide the direction of the pass to a position favourable to the defence.
2. Guard against the return pass after the ball is brought into play.
3. Double-team the ball-handler with the Container in the 1st Trap Area to the left or right.
4. Steal the ball if the Container forces the dribbler to reverse.
5. Intercept the mid-court area when the ball is in the 2nd Trap Area.
Containers (6 and 7)
1. Guide the direction of the ball-handler into the first trap, making use of the sideline as additional defence.
2. Contain the dribbler by preventing his progression down the sidelines. Try to force him into a reverse dribble, but never allow access down the sideline.
3. With the help of the Chaser, double-team the ball-handler in the 1st Trap Area.
4. If the ball is moved up the sideline, effect the double-team with the Interceptor in the 2nd Trap Area.
5. Deny the next pass possibility around the free-throw line area when the ball is in the 1st Trap Area opposite.
6. Intercept the back-court area when the ball is in the 2nd Trap Area opposite.
Interceptor (8)
1. Be aware of all offensive players in the area and be prepared to cover the full width of the court.
2. Intercept all short and long passes between the free-throw and half-way lines.

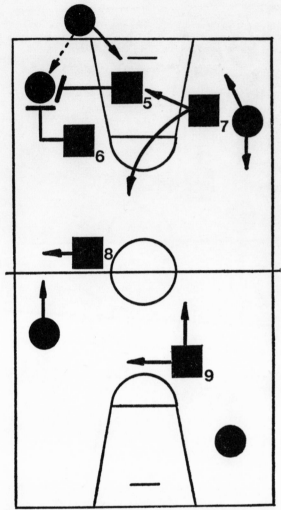

39. Full-court zone press: player responsibilities I

3. If the ball is moved up the sideline, intercept and effect the double-team with the help of the Container in the 2nd Trap Area.

4. Protect the under-basket area if the ball crosses the half-way line.

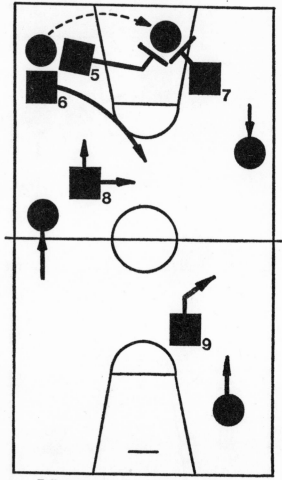

40.   Full-court zone press: player responsibilities II

5. Communicate the whereabouts of all offensive players to the Containers.

Protector (9)

1. Assist the Interceptor in protecting the mid-court area.
2. Protect the basket area against long passes.
3. Protect the basket against uncontested lay-up shots if the press fails.

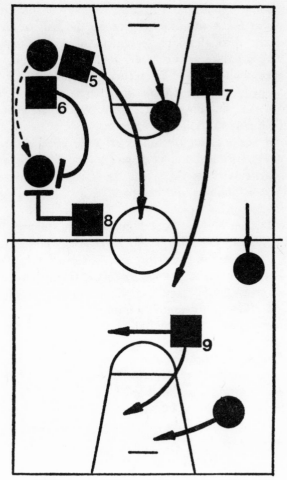

41. Full-court zone press: player responsibilities III

4. Communicate the whereabouts of all offensive players to the Interceptor.

For the press to be effective, good footwork, balance and speed of movement are essential. Each player should be sold on the idea of the press, always stressing the importance of aggressiveness, hustle, anticipation and proper floor balance. In order to overcome the problem of fouling, set the traps away from the Game Officials and instil in the players that the press is designed to make the offence give up the ball by throwing bad passes and through floor violations. Don't expect to steal the ball at every situation as this causes fouling by reaching in, but play defence with the feet by securing proper court position. The double-teamers should wave their hands and arms to force a high lob pass, but never reach in or slap down on the ball – they should play the ball from underneath.

A second variation of the full-court zone press is the 2–2–1 alignment. The same basic principles apply, but this arrangement is particularly useful when the Containers are having difficulties in containing the ball-handler in the 1st Trap Area of the 1–2–1–1 press.

Players (4) and (7) would become Chasers, players (6) and (8) would become Containers and Interceptors combined, and player (9) would be the Protector. The Chasers attempt to deny. the ball being thrown in-bounds by facing their opponents and forcing an over-the-top pass, which offers the opportunity of interception. Players (6) and (8) would continually be looking for the interception or, as the ball is put into play, contain the ball-handler whilst the double-team is effected with the nearest Chaser. From this point on, the application is the same as for the 1–2–1–1 press, as player (8) would recover to the mid-court area and take on the role of Interceptor. At all times the ball-handler would be forced to the sidelines and the centre court area denied.

8. Team Coaching

PRACTICE SESSIONS

Teams have many problems to face when it comes to the organisation of practice sessions. At the present time, the majority of teams have to rely on educational facilities in order to play, and are unable to start practice for the new season until schools open for the new academic year; although the use of outdoor courts (where in existence) would be a great help during the summer months and the new sports centres springing up around the country enable better facilities to be used.

Consequently, teams usually start practice for the new season some time in September and have only four weeks, at the most, in which to prepare before leagues get under way in October.

During these four weeks, many teams have only a 70 x 40 ft school gymnasium available to them on one evening each week for two hours' duration. Some teams are more fortunate in being able to hold practice sessions twice weekly (four hours).

This two-hour practice period is usually between 7 and 9 p.m., but never starts until all players have arrived, so that it may be 7.30 p.m. before anything constructive is attempted. By 9 p.m. the caretaker is usually complaining of late hours and waiting to lock up, so practice has to cease at 8.45 p.m. in order that the premises can be cleared by 9 p.m. – resulting in $1\frac{1}{4}$ hours' actual practice, or for those more fortunate, $2\frac{1}{2}$ hours' practice per week.

If basketball is to progress and a higher standard achieved, teams should strive to obtain better playing facilities and players should be encouraged to attend practices punctually and regularly. Each session should be planned to make full use of the time available. It is impossible to devote a great deal of this time to physical fitness training specifically, otherwise time spent on the techniques and skills of the game would be insufficient for the overall improvement of players. Even so, physical fitness is extremely important in basketball, and where time is not available for this activity players should be encouraged to work on their own.

Each practice session should be planned, and conditioning can play an important part. The use of fast-break practices will not only help the players assimilate game conditions, but will also help them physically to get into shape and condition for the game itself; but remember the old adage: 'A good sweat does not necessarily constitute a good session.'

TEAM OBJECTIVES

No game is ever started with a poorly inflated ball and, similarly, no coach should start a game with a poorly prepared team. Before players step on to the practice floor, each coach should have prepared the team objectives for the season. From the previous season's experiences, he should know the individual ability of his players, their attributes, weaknesses and the sort of competition they will be playing against during the coming season, and should plan his team requirements before practice begins.

In general, each team should develop the following minimum objectives:

1. *To develop three types of Defence*
(a) Man-to-man defence
(b) Zone defence
(c) Pressing defence (half- or full-court). Man-to-man should be the basic form of defence, whilst the others would be used where the situation demands.

2. *To develop three styles of Offence*
(a) Against man-to-man defence/or combination offence,
(b) Against zone defence/to cater for both man-to-man and zone

13. Jump ball situation. Note the positions of Rae (9) and Gattorna (11). Positional play by No. 11 has caused two players to defend him (No. 7 and team mate). Wilson Panthers v. Pentland

14. West Midlands' break out play at an out-of-bounds situation. West Midlands v. England U. 19 Squad

(c) Against the press.

3. *Immediate reaction to the Change of Possession* – one of the most important factors in the game.

(a) Instant defensive obedience

(b) Instant offensive obedience – fast break.

4. *To develop a controlled Fast Break* creating 2-on-1 and 3-on-2 situations.

5. *To develop a Stall Play* to protect the lead at the end of a game or to manoeuvre for the last shot in the dying seconds of a half or game.

6. *To develop organised Plays* at the following game situations :

(a) Tip-off at beginning of game and start of second-half

(b) Jump-ball at each free-throw restraining circle

(c) Defensive and offensive free-throws

(d) Out-of-bounds ball in the front court and half-way line.

Obviously it would be an impossiblity to become highly skilled in these objectives during the short time available at the beginning of the season before matches commence. These objectives should be developed over the season, and will no doubt take many more than one season to perfect. But the pursuit of these objectives is within the capabilities of most teams, as in many cases the turnover of personnel is very slight and a coach should be able to build on the previous seasons' experiences each year.

PLAYER ROLES

As a player begins to develop and acquires the necessary skills of the game, he starts to specialise and favour a particular position on court (offensively). This should be done through the guidance of his coach, who will take into consideration all his other attributes as a player. If he is tall and strong, he may be coached to play the Post. If he is tall, but not so well built, he may be used as a Forward. But whatever is decided, it is the coach's decision and should fall in line with his philosophy of the game.

Once players have been categorised into playing positions, they should obtain as much practice as possible in these positions, and under 'Organisation of Practice' it will be seen how this may be achieved.

F

ORGANISATION OF PRACTICE

Having stated that each practice session should be carefully planned beforehand, and having discovered that all players do not arrive at the training venue on time, it is necessary to prepare a programme with the first part of the session designed to include each player in a particular activity as he arrives.

The next part of the training session could be used to help to prepare the team physically, and the remaining time devoted to the Team Objectives already outlined.

A training scheme is detailed below and is based on a weekly or twice weekly session of two hours' duration.

7.00 to 7.30 p.m. Individual Shooting Assignments.
7.30 to 7.40 p.m. Pressure Training – Fitness.
7.40 to 8.00 p.m. Shooting Practice (controlled).
8.00 to 8.40 p.m. Individual Techniques and Pre-Tactical Play.
8.40 to 9.00 p.m. Scrimmage (Team Tactics – controlled).

I. INDIVIDUAL SHOOTING ASSIGNMENTS (30 min.)

Under match conditions, the winning team is the one which has scored the most points, and as shooting ability plays a major role leading to this end result, the first 30 minutes of practice could be devoted to this on an organised individual basis.

The coach should always be the first to arrive at practice and set each player as he arrives a task to perform, depending on his role in the game. This may be a certain number of shots scored from his particular position on court. In this way, players are immediately put to work and the coach is able to assist each player constructively during this period.

Post Players

These players would shoot and score, say 25 jump shots, 25 left-hand hook shots, 25 right-hand hook shots and 25 'figure-eight' shots, all from in and around the free-throw area.

'Figure-Eight' Shooting – This term is used simply to describe the player's movement whilst performing this practice. The player initially stands under and slightly to one side of the basket and jumps off his left leg, shooting with the right hand. Collects the rebound, strides to his left and jumps off his right leg, shooting with his left hand. Collects the rebound, strides to his right ... and so on, performing the practice with a continuous fluent motion until the required number of shots have been scored. A very good practice for under-basket shooting, making use of either hand.

Guards and Forwards

These players would shoot and score, say 50 shots from either the right- or left-hand side of the court and 50 shots from out front. These players to some degree are interchangeable and should, therefore, be able to score from all these positions.

Ideally, players are required to work in pairs, although the system can operate quite successfully in three's and four's. If working in pairs, one player would rebound all shots and could also practise tipping, whilst the shooter would move to a slightly different position in readiness to receive the ball for his next shot and count the shots scored. On completion, the roles would be reversed. If working in a team, each player would count his own shots scored and rotate to rebound in turn. Players should be encouraged to shoot on the spot and on no account should they be allowed to bounce the ball for the sake of bouncing it before shooting, as this very soon becomes habit-forming and will present difficulties in the game situation.

An alternative for this initial session would be to have the players pair off as they arrive and go 1-on-1 from their respective positions on court. This activity can be performed in two ways:

(a) *1-on-1* (*Shooting bias*): Each player would rebound his own shot and stay at the basket until he has scored. The ball is then passed to his colleague who has placed himself in a position from which he would immediately shoot on receiving the ball, whilst the passer rushes at the shooter to put pressure on the shot. As the shot is released, the shooter follows the ball to rebound, whilst the passer, after trying to block the initial shot, remains in the outer court area and positions himself in readiness to receive the ball for his next shot. No blocking out is performed by the defensive player, he merely puts pressure on the shooter. The shooter practises spot shooting under the threat of an advancing defensive player and backs this up by following his shot to rebound. Each player would position himself to shoot from his particular area on court and would generally take jump shots. He would be permitted to fake and use a short drive before shooting if the defence advanced quickly, but would not be allowed to take lay-up shots.

(b) *1-on-1 (Offence and Defence)*: After practising the shooting-biased 1-on-1 play for a period of time, or as more players arrive full offence and defence may be practised in the 1-on-1 situation. An offensive player with the ball would position himself, along with a defensive player, in his particular area on court and then attempt to score by going 1-on-1.

The defence attempts to stop him scoring by good positional defence, and as the shot is taken both players would rebound. This practice could be made competitive by seeing which player was first to score, say 15 baskets, and could be performed from any position on court.

2. PRESSURE TRAINING-FITNESS (10 minutes)
As has been stated earlier, it is not possible in the time available to spend much time in the physical preparation of the players in terms of fitness. Players should be encouraged towards peak physical fitness by giving them schedules to work on in their own time away from the basketball court, and where possible by encouraging them to take up weight training in the close season to build up their strength.

A short period of pressure training during each session can help players to get in physical shape for the game, and detailed below is a schedule which can be performed either on or off the basketball court. It can also be inserted anywhere in the practice session, and some coaches may prefer to insert it at the very end of the session.

1. 6 Shuttle runs, followed by 15 seconds' rest.
2. Press-ups for 30 seconds, followed by 15 seconds' rest.

3. 6 Shuttle runs, followed by 15 seconds' rest.
4. Jumps for 30 seconds, followed by 15 seconds' rest.
5. 6 Shuttle runs, followed by 15 seconds' rest.
6. Trunk curls for 30 seconds, followed by 15 seconds' rest.
7. 6 Shuttle runs.

Each task should be performed at maximum effort if players are to gain any benefit. Shuttle runs are sprints across the breadth of a basketball court (14–15 m) going flat out.

The number of press-ups should be counted by each individual, so that a measure of improvement can be assessed at each session.

Jumps: players are required to jump as high as they can repetitively at full stretch with both arms, preferably beneath some object they can reach for (e.g. basket), and again mentally record the number performed.

Trunk curls should be done as rapidly as possible and again the number noted.

Where players are performing this schedule on their own and have no timing device, they should do at least 25 each of press-ups, jumps and trunk curls, and count what is considered to be 15 seconds' rest between each task. The shuttle run distance can be measured out and should present no difficulty in setting up.

3. SHOOTING PRACTICE (20 minutes)

Following the Pressure Training, the players should immediately go into their controlled shooting practice, which applies pressure on each individual, as accuracy and success are required whilst they are still in a fatigued state. Detailed below is a controlled shooting schedule organised in two lanes. One lane shooting, the other lane rebounding and feeding the ball out to the next player shooting.

(a) 20 Right-hand lay-ups scored
(b) 20 Left-hand lay-ups scored
(c) 20 Right-hand hook shots scored
(d) 20 Left-hand hook shots scored
(e) 20 Lay-ups scored (middle court)

(f) 20 Jump shots scored (middle court)

(g) 100 Tips of the ball on the backboard

In order to provide an element of competition during this shooting practice, divide the players into two groups.

As the pressure training activity is completed, the two groups would immediately go into the shooting practice (one group at each end of the court) and the first group to complete the schedule would be the winners, with the losing group being required to pay some form of penalty, like running twenty laps of the gymnasium at the end of the evening. Competition of this kind makes the players concentrate and provides for better shooting accuracy whilst in a fatigued state, as they do not usually want to run laps and therefore try harder for success.

Alternatively, after completing the pressure training, players could be divided up into groups of two, three, four, etc., and complete a different shooting schedule as follows: On a given signal, each group would compete against each other to score ten baskets from ten predetermined spots on the floor. Seven inside positions from around the free-throw area and three outside positions (both corners and top of the free-throw area) to give a total of 100 baskets scored. Again they would be shooting in a semi-fatigued state and the element of competition, with suitable penalties for losing, would help to create the pressures of the game situation.

4. INDIVIDUAL TECHNIQUES AND PRE-TACTICAL PLAY
(40 minutes)

During this period of the practice session, the players should perform those skills related to the development of the individual and team objectives set out earlier. Practices should be devised to provide an environment as near to the game situation as possible in order that the transfer of skill from practice to the real thing is kept to a minimum. When developing offensive techniques, introduce an element of defence at the earliest opportunity, and equal time should be spent developing both offensive and defensive techniques during this period.

Theoretically, if each team in a 40-minute game had equal

possession of the ball, each team would be spending half the game (20 minutes) playing defence and should, therefore, be spending at least this proportion of time on the development of defence during practice. This allocation of time may be split even further when it is considered that possession of the ball is divided between five players, i.e. each player has possession of the ball for only one-fifth (4 minutes) of its offensive allocation in the game. All players, therefore, spend four-fifths (16 minutes) of each game on offence without the ball and 20 minutes on defence (one-fifth of which is spent defending the player with the ball). From this little exercise, it can be seen how important defence is to the overall success of the team and how important it is for each individual, offensively and defensively, to be able to work in the game without the ball.

Practices should include those individual and pre-tactical skills outlined in earlier chapters, and once the coach has decided on his team objectives, these should be broken down in order that some facet of the game may be practised at each session, as it would be impossible for all the objectives to be developed at once. It may be that 'Man-to-Man Offence and Defence' be the theme at the first session, followed by 'Zone Offence and Defence' at the second and 'Fast-Break Attack and Defence' at the third, and so on until all the objectives have been covered. The team may first concentrate on man-to-man defence and only consider introducing a zone defence in practice when the team has competently mastered the individual techniques of the former, but whatever is decided, the coach should plan each session and emphasise, during this period, those skills which are necessary for the overall improvement of the individual players and team.

When developing the team offence, which is made up of one-, two-and three-man plays, devise practices based on the offensive system which will provide repetitive practice. Introduce defensive players early in the practice and have both the offence and defence working at the same time to provide 1-on-1, 2-on-2 and 3-on-3 situations.

For example, it may be that a Guard-to-Forward relationship occurs as part of a team's man-to-man offence and this needs to be practised in isolation from the other plays. This may be organised as described in Chapter 4, and may even be further expanded to include a Post player, thus creating a 3-on-3 situation. Each aspect of the offence could be treated in the same way, with some form of rotation to ensure that each player gets an opportunity to play in each position.

The fast-break may also be organised during this period, which is built up of 2-on-1 and 3-on-2 situations as outlined in a previous chapter, and also acts as a very good conditioner. The session could be ended by getting each player to shoot free-throws, with one lap being run for each free-throw missed.

5. SCRIMMAGE – TEAM TACTICS (20 minutes)

This is the period during which the isolated one- two- and three-man plays are put together to form the basic team-offence and defence, and all other facets of team plays are practised.

Many teams are content during practice to select two teams, throw a ball up and play a game for the whole session, hoping some measure of improvement will take place if they do it often enough. Undoubtedly, improvement will occur in time to a certain degree, but habits will also occur and if sessions are not planned and coached correctly, much time is wasted and players are not able to develop to their full potential.

Where scrimmaging is introduced in practice, it should be planned and controlled. It provides an ideal opportunity for the offence to be practised on a team basis and for the defence to co-ordinate its moves collectively. Controlled play allows the coach to further the team's objectives, as each situation provides an opportunity for developing some aspect of the game, whether it be the immediate recognition of change in possession offensively or defensively, setting up an out-of-bounds play, or developing the full-court press.

(a) *Half-Court Scrimmaging:* Unless the fast break or some form of full-court press is being practised, it is better to develop a team's offence and defence on a half-court basis, using only one basket. This obviates a certain amount of time wasting when moving players from one end of the court to the other, and it is also difficult to control the offence and defence of two teams at the same time.

The coach should concentrate on the players of one team and a particular aspect of the game with that team. For example, the coach may concentrate on the team's offence against a man-to-man defence and at this stage he would not be too concerned with the finer points of the defence, but would be controlling the offence to ensure that the correct plays were being executed and that the players were reading the situations correctly and using the right options. The offence would bring the ball in play at the half-way line, and each time there is a breakdown in play this would be corrected and possession returned to the offensive team.

If the teams were fairly evenly matched, this half-court scrimmage could be made competitive by allowing each team on offence five or six attempts at scoring before they changed round to give the defensive team an opportunity to play on offence. In this way it is possible for twenty players (two teams at each basket) to scrimmage at the same time, and additional players may be substituted in the games as required. Even though the scrimmaging may be competitive, the coach should not hesitate to stop the game at any point to make necessary corrections to the offensive team's play, as half-court scrimmaging should be designed to offer repetitive practice in a controlled situation.

The whole court may be combined with a half-court scrimmage when practising defence, as allied to this aspect of the game is the important factor of recognising the change in possession and the fast break.

One team would be playing half-court offence whilst the coach would be controlling the defensive play of the other team. Immediately the defensive team gained possession of the ball from the field of play, it would fast break and attempt to score in the other basket; whilst the team which had lost possession would attempt to stop the break.

All players would remain at the fast-break end of the court and the ball be given back to the offensive team for the practice to begin again. If the offence score, they retain possession, with the defensive team only being permitted to fast break if they obtain the ball from a rebound or interception. By organising the practice in this way, the players are encouraged to play defence knowing they have the opportunity of fast breaking when they gain possession of the ball. At all times the practice is controlled by the coach, who should be critically examining the defensive role of the team and each player.

Half-court scrimmaging would also provide an ideal opportunity for developing organised plays when the ball is out-of-bounds, and in jump-ball or free-throw situations.

(b) *Conditioned Scrimmage:* The whole court is generally used when playing a conditioned game, which limits the actions of the two teams involved and highlights some particular aspect of the game.

With beginners, the coach may decide to cut out dribbling in order to create player movement to receive the ball and emphasise better passing. He may restrict shooting to jump shots only, or permit shots to be taken only from outside the 3-second area to assist the development in outside shooting and to create more rebound situations; or he may have both teams playing man-to-man defence and allow under-basket shots only to help the teams develop cutting and screen plays.

Many aspects of the game can be conditioned in this way to illustrate the techniques involved, and the coach should be in full control, stopping the game where necessary to correct errors and point out other possibilities. This form of scrimmage provides a good opportunity for beginners and developing players to put into practice those individual skills learnt earlier in the session, without having the complication of having to remember and do everything at once.

BENCH COACHING

ORGANISATION

The team benches are located to the right and left of the Table Officials on which are seated the teams and team officials. The coach is responsible for all personnel on his team bench, and in order to exercise control and communicative efficiency the bench layout should be organised.

The coach should generally be seated near the end of the bench nearest the Table Officials, as he has to communicate with the scorer when requesting time-outs and substitutions. Between the coach and the team should be left a space for use by the substitutes going into or coming out of the game, in order that they may be briefed.

If the team has an assistant coach, he should be the first one in line after the space, followed by the team. In this position he is in direct contact with the coach to provide any information necessary, and is also on hand during the briefing of substitutes. If the team is fortunate in having an assistant coach and a Manager, the assistant coach should take up the same position, whilst the Manager sits at the end nearest the table next to the coach to assist with the technical details of the game (Diagram 42).

42. Organisation of the coach's bench

ASSISTANT COACH

During the game the assistant coach is responsible to the coach and should help by offering advice and comments on the game. He may be asked to concentrate on the individual offensive and defensive attributes and weaknesses of the team and offer advice thereon, whilst the coach views the game as a whole and concentrates on the strategies of the opposition. In this way, the game is analysed in more depth and offers greater coverage.

The assistant coach should keep a record of the individual fouls committed by both teams and inform the coach immediately a player has committed three, as he may want to get him out of the game. The coach also wants to know which opposition players are on four fouls, as he may want to play on this weakness.

A record of the number of time-outs by both teams during the second-half should also be kept, as this is very important during the latter stages of a game if the score is close. During the half-time interval, the coach should be presented with the foul situation of both teams and which opposition players are doing the most damage.

If a team has additional personnel to call on, they should be put to good use charting the shots taken, offensive and defensive rebounding, number of turnovers, etc., which can be viewed during the interval and assist in planning second-half strategy. These persons may be seated on the end of the team bench or directly behind it.

Each team should have a medical bag containing at least those items necessary for the prevention and treatment of basketball injuries, and this should be made available at the team bench during games in order to administer any first-aid required. It is also worth while having a cold wet towel available to refresh the players during time-outs, and a container holding some form of thirst-quencher.

STRATEGIES

Team strategy begins the moment practices commence, but game strategy begins at the start of the game. As game time arrives the team should be in a state of readiness, having been prepared in offence and defence during practice to meet all contingencies.

PRE-GAME STRATEGY

During the 3 minutes before the game starts, the coach should call his team together and highlight the tactical aspects previously discussed in depth in the dressing-room, and give any last minute instructions to individuals and the team. As it is also important that the substitutes hear what the coach has to say, this can be organised as shown in Diagram 43. The starting five are seated on the bench with the coach out front, and the

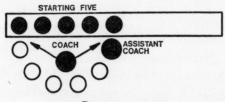

43. Pre-game strategy

substitutes are grouped around the coach in a semi-circle, thus ensuring that the undivided attention of all players is given to the coach.

At this session the coach should reiterate the defence to be played, and issue any individual instructions to the players concerning either their own defence or the offensive manoeuvres of the opposition. The offensive alignment will depend a great deal on the opposition's defence, and the team should be instructed to assess the situation immediately on their first offensive manoeuvre down court and establish their offensive play accordingly. If in doubt as to what the defence is playing, run a player towards the basket and through the defence. If he is followed by the same player throughout, it can be safely assumed that man-to-man is the defence and the offence can be organised accordingly.

Refresh the players' minds on fast-break policy and rebounding responsibilities. Decide who is jumping for the tip-off and whether a play is to be used for an attempt at basket or, if unsure of the outcome, whether to attempt for possession only or set up defensive measures.

The coach should always carry a stick of chalk in his pocket to sketch diagrams of plays, as this leads to better comprehension by the players.

GAME STRATEGY

As the game commences, the coach should first concentrate on the opposition. Examine their defensive formation for weaknesses or other defects that can be taken advantage of; if they are strong down one side of the court, emphasise the offence down the other; shoot from the sides where the strongest rebounders are located to pull them away from the basket and if a big player is defended by a shorter one, send him to the basket where this advantage can be put to good use. He should examine their offensive alignment and make any adjustments in defence necessary. Perhaps the corners or out front need more protection, and if playing a zone defence, a change in its formation may provide the necessary emphasis. If playing a man-to-man defence, some adjustments may be required to contain certain opposition personnel which can be effected by switching defensive assignments.

Good strategy demands proper use of substitutes and time-outs. Through wise substitutions, a coach can strengthen his team's overall play, as he should know every player's ability, condition, strengths and weaknesses, and where they are most effective.

TIME-OUTS

Each team is permitted two time-outs during each half of play and one during each period of extra time. They should be used wisely and always for a reason – they should not be wasted.

The time-out is one of the greatest weapons at the disposal of a coach during a game, and is requested by the coach going in person to the scorer and asking clearly for a 'time-out'. Each time-out lasts for a maximum of one minute, during which time the coach has the opportunity of talking with the team and making any changes he deems necessary in game strategy. Substitutions may also be made during a time-out.

In the game situation the time-out offers the finest means of communication between players and coach; during the second-half, at least one time-out should be reserved for the last few minutes of play in order that special instructions may be given in the event of a close game.

WHEN TO CALL A TIME-OUT

1. Whenever a defensive or offensive change in strategy is necessary, which cannot be communicated whilst the game is in progress.

2. Whenever the opposition get 'hot' and the offensive surge has to be stopped.

3. Whenever the team hits a 'cold' spell on offence and adjustments are needed to shake off the slump.

4. To correct repeated mistakes made by the team, defensively or offensively. When a player makes repeated mistakes, substitute him.

5. To rest a team when no substitutes are available or not wanted at that stage in the game.

6. To set up strategic plays during the dying minutes of the game.

7. Don't use a time-out for one player, substitute him.

SUBSTITUTIONS

A team may substitute players during the game at any of the following situations:

(a) When a held ball has been called, except for that player involved in the jump.

(b) When a foul has been called.

(c) When a time-out has been granted.

(d) When the game has been stopped by the Game Officials for any other reason.

(e) Following a violation, but only by the team which has possession of the ball on the sideline. If this occurs, the opposition may then also substitute. Substitutions are requested by the coach and all players must report to the scorer and remain at the table on the seating provided, until the occasion arises for them to enter the game. Each substitute should be dressed ready to enter the game immediately – track suits should be off, although the top may be draped over a player's shoulders to keep him warm. Teams may substitute up to five players at any one time, but the whole procedure should not take more than 20 seconds regardless of the number of substitutions effected by the team.

WHEN TO SUBSTITUTE

1. Generally, whenever a player commits three fouls during the first-half and whenever a player has four at any time, except

possibly during the last few minutes of play. Save these players, they may be needed late in the game.

2. Whenever a player is ill, tired or injured.

3. Whenever a player is having an 'off-night' shooting, after being given the chance to settle down. He can always be put back in the game later.

4. Whenever a player is mis-matched with his opponent on defence and the switching of assignments won't help.

5. Whenever a player is having a poor game on defence and is continually making mistakes.

6. Whenever a team needs either more scoring power or defensive strength and there is a player on the bench who can help.

7. Whenever a defensive specialist is required on one of the opposition, and a player on the bench can be instructed to fill this role.

8. Whenever a team has built up a lead and offers the opportunity for those players on the bench who don't play too often, to get in the game and gain experience.

9. Whenever the opposition are pressing and better ball-handlers are needed in the game.

10. Use a substitute to communicate with the team during the dying stages of the game when no time-outs are left.

11. During the dying seconds when the scores are close and a jump-ball situation is called between any two players. Send in the big man to take the tip.

12. When less than 30 seconds of play are remaining and the team is leading by a few points, with the opposition in possession of the ball. Send in the better defensive players to protect the lead.

HALF-TIME STRATEGY

The half-time interval is of 10 minutes' duration, unless local conditions warrant an increase in time to 15 minutes.

This is an important stage in the game where first-half strategies can be reviewed and second-half strategies formulated. When possible, the team should go somewhere quiet (usually the dressing-room) where they can relax for a few minutes and take care of their pressing needs.

The coach should examine any charts that have been made of the game and let the players know the foul situation of both teams and which opposition players have been doing most scoring. The opponent's offence should be reviewed and any necessary adjustments made to the team's defence. The second-half starting five should be announced and any necessary instructions given. The last 4 or 5 minutes of the interval should be spent by the players shooting baskets to loosen up for the start of the second-half. Just prior to the second-half starting, the players should again be grouped at the team bench to receive any last-minute instructions from the coach.

END-OF-GAME STRATEGIES

End-of-game strategy depends entirely on the relationship of the scores between the two teams and how much time is remaining in the game. If there is a large points margin between the two teams, there is very little the coach or players can do about it late in the game. Strategy should have been formulated earlier in the match to have alleviated this situation.

1. FREE-THROW OR POSSESSION OPTION

During the last few minutes of the game and with the scores close, one of the biggest problems facing the coach is whether or not to shoot free-throws or maintain possession of the ball. Firstly the coach should have ensured that whoever is the Court Captain at the time, looks immediately to the coach for instructions whenever this situation occurs. The Court Captain should concentrate on his playing responsibilities and leave these decisions to the coach.

In the following situations it is assumed that the player awarded shots is a reasonable free-throw shooter.

(a) If two or more points in the lead at any time during this period, shoot the free-throws, as the opposition must then score twice either to tie or take the lead.

(b) If one point in the lead and just over 30 seconds remains, take possession and work for the good shot.

(c) If the scores are tied or one point in the lead, and less than

30 seconds but more than 5 seconds remains, take possession of the ball and play for the last shot. If less than 5 seconds remains, shoot the free-throws and pressure the rebounder or the in-bounds pass, whichever the case may be, to delay the opposition from getting the ball down court.

(d) In a free-throw situation with 10 seconds or less remaining and still two points down after the first throw, aim at the front rim of the basket with the second shot and try for the return rebound. To have scored from the foul-line would have put the team still one point behind, and in all probability the opposition would have stalled the ball until time ran out. At all times when a team is trailing, shoot the free-throws.

2. APPLY PRESSURE

If a team is trailing by more than ten points with less than 10 minutes remaining in the game, consider using a half- or full-court press to upset the rythm of the opposition's offence. With only a few minutes remaining and ten points down, the trailing team must press, especially when the opponents are opting for possession instead of shooting free-throws, as this tends to favour the defence by producing a 5-on-4 situation with an opponent out-of-bounds attempting to put the ball in play.

3. STALL OFFENCE

When a team is leading during the final 30 seconds of play in a close match and they have possession of the ball, a stall (or freeze) play should be used to run out the clock. Possession of the ball should be retained the whole time. If the opposition repeatedly foul, continue to opt for possession and only consider shooting if 5 seconds or less is remaining.

4. LAST SHOT SITUATION

(a) When a team in possession of the ball is one or two points down or the scores are tied with less than 30 seconds remaining, it should play for the last shot. This should be taken with about 6 seconds remaining in order to leave sufficient time for the team to gain one or two offensive tips if the shot is unsuccessful. The shot taken should result from a drive to the basket, as the defence will either allow the drive or possibly foul in the process of attempting to stop the shot.

In either case, the percentages are greatly in favour of the offensive player and the ensuing shots could possibly win the game. If leading in this situation, maintain possession until time runs out or set up the best shooter for a good shot in the dying seconds.

(b) If a team has possession of the ball out-of-bounds in its own half with less than 5 seconds remaining, either free a player by the use of screens deep in the opponent's territory to receive a long pass and immediate shot, or throw a long high ball into the under-basket area for the offence to tip. Even with one second remaining the latter is possible, as the game clock is not started until touched by a player on court, giving sufficient time for a tip at basket.

WATCHING THE GAME

When the beginner goes to see a match, particularly one from the National League, or an International match, it presents a wonderful opportunity for learning more about the game. It is a fact in teaching that beginners in any physical activity are helped in their learning of skills by seeing a good demonstration of those skills. It would therefore be to the advantage of all beginners if, when seeing the matches, they could have some guidance in what to look for.

In the earlier chapters of this book the authors have given guides and check points relevant to the specific individual skills. Armed with some knowledge of the points mentioned, the beginner can observe the players on the court and look at the style and method of execution of individual skills. He can note why players are successful or unsuccessful in their attempts to use the skills they have, whether it concerns footwork in getting free, arm action in shooting, type of dribble used in beating a defender, or the type of pass used in a particular situation. Whilst looking at the techniques, the beginner may also form his own opinion as to whether the individuals are utilising the skills that they have to the full.

It is also very good for the beginner to become involved in analysing the game whilst it is in progress, the depth to which he can go being relative to his experience. This will help in showing what part an individual plays in the whole performance of the team.

Firstly, it is better to look at both teams' defensive performances. Establishing which type of defence each team is playing should be followed by an assessment of whether each is doing its job. Having found out which type of defence each team is playing, the next thing to look for would be the offensive manoeuvres used in trying to break down the defences. Usually this would be enough for the beginner, but if a more experienced spectator wishes to analyse further, then references should be made to the sections on methods of offence, and comparisons made to see if the teams are using the accepted basis for attacking the various forms of defence.

Beginners can also learn a lot about the application of the rules of basketball from watching big games. Referees are trained to see that the game is played within the rules, and watching Grade One and International referees will give the best demonstration of what is permissible and what is not.

Beginner coaches who are on the long climb to the top should find the information given so far, relevant but inadequate. Their observations should go much deeper. If they are observing in order to learn more about the game, then assessing the strengths and weaknesses of the defensive and offensive deployments should lead into what changes can be made to improve team performance. Also it would be useful to speculate why the coaches make the changes they do during the game, either the changes in personnel or the changes in tactics.

It is always easy to sit and criticise other coaches during games, so the beginner coach would be better advised to look on the positive side when getting involved, and instead of making a mental note that the coach should have done this or that, an examination of *why* the coach did what he did would be more fruitful. Even top coaches get into the bad habit of criticising each other without trying to find out reasons, and the beginner coach can set new trends by looking at the good things that coaches do, thus being constructive and not destructive.

Coaching basketball is a matter of backing one's own judgement, and not always are the right decisions made. Spectators, in fact, can do their 'coaching' from the gallery and do not have to justify their decisions, neither do they lose the games. Even so they are 'coaching' in a sense, and are welcomed to the fold. It would be nicer to see more of them on the bench, though, and perhaps through these few words on how to look at the game, more may take up the challenge and be practical coaches rather than theoretical onlookers.

Index

Index